JESUS CONFRONTS LIFE'S ISSUES

Joseph D. Ban

JUDSON PRESS, Valley Forge

JESUS CONFRONTS LIFE'S ISSUES

Copyright © 1972
Judson Press, Valley Forge, Pa. 19481
Third Printing, 1974

Except where otherwise indicated, the Bible quotations in this volume are in accordance with the Revised Standard Version of the Bible, copyright © 1946 and 1952, by the Division of Christian Education of the National Council of the Churches of Christ in the United States of America, and are used by permission.

Other versions used are:

The New English Bible. Copyright © The Delegates of the Oxford University Press and The Syndics of the Cambridge University Press, 1961, 1971.

Today's English Version of the New Testament. Copyright © American Bible Society, 1966.

New Testament in Modern English © J. B. Phillips, 1958. Used by permission of the Macmillan Company and Geoffrey Bles, Ltd.

International Standard Book No. 0-8170-0547-1
Library of Congress Catalog Card No. 73-182245

Printed in the U.S.A.

CONTENTS

INTRODUCTION

How did Jesus handle the crisis situations in his own earthly life? We can find today in Jesus' responses some healthy clues for handling life when we feel torn asunder. The Christian message is good news, especially for persons who recognize that they are up against the crunching experiences of life. A crisis is a particular turning point in a series of human episodes. How each of us handles such critical moments determines the direction of future events. A crisis sometimes gathers past events together in such a climactic way that serious decisions can no longer be avoided.

The good news is any word or action that brings a new sense that life is good and that human experience does have purpose and meaning. The Christian is one who has experienced the freedom which comes with recognizing God as the liberator made visible in Jesus Christ.

As you read these pages, you may find help in more adequately handling your own crises. These chapters describe how Jesus worked through some of the life-shaping challenges that confronted him in his real life.

This is not a scholarly treatise on the life of Jesus, though I have tried consistently to make use of the best scholarship available. The ideas you will find here have been formed by a theology which is quite orthodox — that is, I have affirmed the person of Christ as the apostle Paul witnessed to Him: "God was in Christ personally reconciling the world to himself . . ." (2 Corinthians 5:19, Phillips). Yet these studies of crucial episodes in Jesus' life do not fall into any orthodox pattern. Life is dynamic, and its experiences often turbulent. My own religious experience has been that Jesus addresses me most directly just where life has roughly treated me.

These chapters are based on certain critical points in the historical life of Yehoshuah of Nazareth. They cover only a part of that life which has so profoundly influenced the course of mankind's history. Many men and women have reflected upon the virile love experienced in communion with Christ Jesus. These pages add to the witness of those influenced by Jesus' life.

5

God's love in Christ has come to me through faith-filled men and women. The pastors of my childhood and youth interpreted to me the wonderful life of Jesus. I would especially acknowledge my debt to Edwin L. Kautz and to my maternal uncle, John Petrusan, both of whom served as missionaries among immigrant Hungarians. Thus they ministered to me, the first child born to a couple who met and married shortly after their arrival in the new land of promise. My friends will recognize the influence of my theological professors, among whom James Rodney Branton and Bernhard Anderson encouraged me in my study of the Bible. My practical application of the Gospel to contemporary events has developed during my association with Charles Lyon Seasholes and Jitsuo Morikawa, to whom I express deep appreciation. May I also express my gratitude to the various congregations in McMinnville, Oregon — Baptist, Methodist, and Presbyterian, who have listened to early beginnings of various chapters. Though some of my ideas were provocative in content, my hearers were open and alert in their response.

It is invigorating to be living one's creative years in a busting-wide-open America and to share these years with three teenagers. They bring to the dinner table conversation their fresh ideas drawn from peaceful protest, the world of Woodstock and Vonnegut, and the turned on and up generation. Sue, Dave, and Debbie continue to wrestle with what it means "to have Christ in our lives" in our kind of world, and their honest facing of conflict has helped me to grow.

I have so much enjoyed working with my wife, Arline, in coauthoring several church school texts that I greatly missed her collaboration in writing this work. Nonetheless, she contributed importantly with personal encouragement as well as in typing the manuscript.

My desire in writing these chapters has been that I might communicate the vital force I have found in life through my continuing awareness of the living presence of God's anointed man. Jesus' own particular history took place in some other time and distant land, but his impact is very real upon me in my own time and present place.

JOSEPH D. BAN

Linfield College
January, 1972

6

1. THE REALITY OF TEMPTATION
Luke 4:1-13

As modern men, we like to pretend that we now live in a temptation-less world. Many contemporary writers would argue that our world is rid of sin. Some college students ridicule guilt as "middle-age, middle-class hang-ups." Temptations are something invented by "dirty old men with crude imaginations." Has mankind reached that high level of actually being liberated from all temptations and guilt? Or are we being straitjacketed by that subtle enticement which insists that temptations no longer really exist?

Jesus had scarcely started his life work before he was forced to undergo a severe trial. It was an enthusiastic young man who rose up out of Jordan's baptismal waters. The Scriptures picture him as "full of the Holy Spirit." A decisive change took place at this point in Jesus' life. During the forty reflective days in the wilderness, he exchanged the gallantry of youth for the gauntness of maturity. This growth came through a testing which wearied his body and tried his spirit.

By observing how Jesus handled this most trying time of his youthful career, we may increase our appreciation of what testing really is. Luke reports that Jesus was first put to the test at the point of a personal need. He was hungry. Then in the second demonic test, Jesus was tempted by an offer of power which would allow him to do everything he so badly wanted to do. The third temptation was an attempt to get Jesus, himself, to check out whether or not God really intended to anoint him as his worldly ambassador.

Jesus' ordeal may be compared to Israel's time of testing in the wilderness. Following their exodus from Egypt, the people wandered for forty years in the barren places. For forty days, Jesus' enthusiasm and endurance were placed to the test. These sore experiences were not only to mark his future but also to measure his capacity. Was this truly God's anointed one? Or must the world wait for another?

Make no mistake, modern reader, the temptations for Jesus were very real indeed. He could not see as far as their outcome. There were before him some big and basic questions which had to be faced. For what kind of work had God set him apart?

7

Was he to try to provide for everybody's personal needs? Or was he to save his people and nation as a hero-rescuer, mounted tall on a white horse? Or was he to win the support of the superstitious crowds by performing awesome magic and grand tricks? Only through a most difficult experience of inward struggle was Jesus able, at last, to see more clearly the way in which God was leading him.

The first temptation which Jesus faced was one of personal need. His experience with John at the Jordan River was a time of dedication. After that he went into the wilderness to sort out and set up his priorities. What did God really want him to do with the remaining years of his life? How could he best follow through on the magnificent moment when he had heard the great tones of God's voice? It had been like a mighty bell ringing down through the canyons of the stars, "You are my own dear Son. I am well pleased with you." He was absolutely certain of God's calling and commission. He was not at all certain just what it was God wanted him to do. Luke tells his readers that while Jesus struggled there in the wilderness, "All that time he had nothing to eat, and at the end of it he was famished" (Luke 4:2, NEB).

As a Jew studying the Holy Scriptures under rabbinical guidance in Nazareth's synagogue, Jesus knew the story of Moses and the desert wanderers (Exodus 16). Each day's manna had provided for their basic needs. Jesus knew that the ravens had cared for Elijah during his long vigil in the desert (1 Kings 17:3-6). Would not some way open up that his own personal needs would be satisfied? And if he could be fed, why not feed the many people of the land who existed on the edge of starvation? In his own famished condition Jesus may have hallucinated on these marvelous prospects: all these people satisfied with good food, and he, himself, once again feeling the satisfaction of a full stomach. After all, had not God promised his people a land of milk and honey? Wasn't the symbol of success a "shining face"? How were the oils of health to flow from the forehead if the belly was an unfilled cavern? For Scripture to be fulfilled, man must have enough to eat. How subtle the argument; how convincing the logic of it all!

It is too neat, too pat. Is man satisfied with three full meals a day? Is life basically a matter of filling these basic needs? What price are we willing to pay to satisfy these fundamental wants?

8

The Devil said to him, "If you are God's Son, order this stone to turn into bread." Here Jesus catches, for the first time, the probably tragic and possibly evil dimension of this rather simple dream. Man's struggle to survive is written into the basic stuff of his physical makeup. Our grandparents said, "It's in your blood." Their grandchildren just as boldly state it: "It's in your genes." Both statements are true. Man, by birth, comes equipped with certain needs and wants. The struggle to stay alive is a fundamental human drive. An adequate diet is a physical want. To meet this need is a very natural desire, indeed.

What's so wrong, then, with Jesus thinking that maybe, as God's anointed representative among people, he might just see to it that this poor mother and that thin little boy just had enough to eat?

Nothing at all. Jesus did try to meet such basic human needs. Later, when his preaching drew great crowds into the countryside, he did provide for them. But Jesus apparently saw a dangerous dimension to all of this. Was he perhaps aware of how the politicians of Rome were already buying off the city crowds by providing for their physical needs and their sensual entertainment? Certainly we are familiar today with contented people who grow fat and lazy watching the televised comedians and athletes but who ignore the news programs because these are too depressing. Jesus was not fighting the urgency to feed starving people. Indeed, again and again he urged his disciples to minister to the needs of the poor. The issue Jesus faced up to here was whether this basic human need was to shape the fundamental character of his life calling.

At this point Jesus was not yet aware that he was to face a number of such tests, nor were the kind of tests he was to face yet apparent to him. This first test was the most simple of them, as we know. Yet its simplicity made it the more treacherous. Jesus lived in a country where hardly 20 percent of the land was suitable for farming. The people depended on the breezes of the Mediterranean to blow in over the coastal chain. These uncertain sea winds brought floods in some years and caused drought in others. Bread was precious to the average Palestinian. The man who could supply a steady source of such daily needs would be a popular man indeed.

Jesus was able to recognize the dangers of this because he remembered Scripture. When Israel had come to the holy

9

mountain, Sinai, God had provided them with some personal instructions. Jesus recalled some of these in his own private hour of soul exploration. He recalled Deuteronomy: "You must remember all that road by which the Lord your God has led you these forty years in the wilderness to humble you, to test you and to discover whether or not it was in your heart to keep his commandments. He humbled you and made you hungry; then he fed you on manna which neither you nor your fathers had known before, to teach you that man cannot live on bread alone but lives by every word that comes from the mouth of the Lord" (Deuteronomy 8:2-3, NEB).

This lesson learned in his Old Testament study was Jesus' reply to the first test. Our present age of technology has yet to learn this lesson. Plenty of evidence shows that we think it is enough to produce more consumable goods. What is the world like, as portrayed in the television and magazine commercials? It is a world of buy and use. You can buy success, and you can use people — or so our ads seem to suggest. Happiness is a high-powered car; so the less principled steal what the visionary young men earn honestly.

Both soon discover that automobiles and motorbikes, especially, fall into the class of goods that rust and are consumed. If we were better students of history, we might be more aware of how shortsighted is our present policy of getting material goods. A suitable home for shelter, an adequate diet, essential clothing, a basic education, needed medical and dental care — all these are basic enough needs. Where modern advertising leads us astray is in claiming that these things are desirable *ends* rather than suitable *means* to higher ends. Advertising persuades us that it is not enough to dress comfortably. We must dress stylishly with a new style for each new season. Clothes stylists have even improved on nature by introducing more new seasons than nature's four original ones. Have you ever tried to buy summer clothing in the summertime?

The automobile is not just transportation. It is a status symbol. It is a measure of your success and is even a substitute in America for the mistress Frenchmen are reputed to keep. The production lines of the U.S., Europe, and Japan turn out modern man's ends. Watch the television ads. Do they claim anything less than a total satisfaction of all your human desires?

Are you still so old-fashioned that you buy a soft drink just to satisfy your thirst? Be up to date: Today's soft drink

10

restores your youth. Join the upbeat generation — you've got a lot to live. What was once only a refreshing drink now is declared to be the fountain of eternal youth. Nothing better demonstrates how dreadfully we have been seduced by the first temptation than the fact that we take television commercials and magazine advertisements seriously.

You know that your old dog Rover is old. But the dog food ads will convince you that Rover can once again be a frisky pup — just switch to a new brand.

If it's true about Rover, how about the two of us? Can't we once again be youthful if we are old, or mature and successful if we are just starting out? That is the miraculous thing about the bread-temptation. It suits whatever your particular needs are. If you are old, we will make you new again. If you are inexperienced and untutored, we will give you instant success. Drive our product. Drink our product. Buy our product. The Devil is still in business. He has just expanded his line of goods. He is limited to bread only in those underdeveloped countries where they cannot yet afford all the fancy, manufactured goods.

To all the pretensions of our modern marketplace come those straightforward words of Jesus and Deuteronomy: "Man cannot live on bread alone!"

But our modern world seems intent on trying to do so. Why? Probably because we are stone-deaf to "every word that comes from the mouth of the Lord." Self-styled "Christian atheists" have been declaring that God has passed away. The arguments of these radical propagandizers rest upon the premise that people no longer believe in God. This supposed fact can also be read in another way: That we no longer hear "every word that comes from the mouth of the Lord" either means that God's voice is stilled by death or that men's hearing is blocked by immorality. Each modern feels free to take his choice.

If training in a rather good school of technology equips a person to better evaluate the limits of technology, then I speak from such a perspective. In my own judgment the "Death of God" school of men were overly optimistic concerning the modern age. They seem to have failed to examine all the evidence. Technology allowed Hitler to exploit the German people's desire for a place in the sun. The Nazis capitalized on the inventions of radio and airplane to saturate the German voters with their political campaigns. The best of Germany's engineer-

11

ing firms designed the gas chambers and ovens used to destroy Germany's Jewish citizens.

Has God's voice really been stilled by death? Or is it man who is morally inert? The temptation to live by earth's bread alone, and without God's bread of life, continues to entice us into sinful and senseless existence.

The second temptation is even more treacherous, for it involves the getting of power in exchange for the giving of one's loyalty. Isn't this the way all human relationships work? I am a citizen of a nation because I pledge it my allegiance. In turn I gain my nation's powerful protection. I am a husband to a wife because I commit myself to her. In response the powers of her personhood are devoted to my well-being.

Part of the temptation lies in the promise of power. Men are fascinated by power. Some observers have commented on how few congressmen and senators ever return to their hometowns after they have lost their political offices in Washington. The sense of power is contagious.

In the nineteenth century, Admiral Dewey and an impressive American fleet forced Japan to open her islands to foreigners. Japan was influenced by the show of power. Equally interesting is the fact that the totally new situation, that of Japan's trade with foreigners, brought a young generation of men to positions of leadership in Japan. Once these young men had experienced power, they were reluctant to give it up. This struggle to gain and hold power is found in every modern nation. Some modern playwright once called success "a bitch-goddess." One wonders what nastier word must be used to describe the dynamic hold exercised by political, military, and financial power.

As a young pastor recently graduated from seminary, I was part of a group of young men who regularly gathered for mutual support and continuing learning. One of our number fled a particularly unhealthy parish situation and entered the air force as a military chaplain. Many months later he visited our city, and our group honored him with a small luncheon. With great enthusiasm he sang the praises of his new employer, the Strategic Air Command. He assured us that he was convinced that he was serving the Prince of Peace in this branch of service whose major mission was to keep the atomic bomb in the skies twenty-four hours each day. As a former noncommissioned and commissioned officer, I could share in his sense of pride in his military unit. But I was shaken by a remark made by another friend as we left the meeting. "How can he be so certain that the ability to destroy the enemy is the surest way to make peace?" I remember how disturbed the question-maker was. Now, after the United States has been engaged in the longest war (undeclared though it may be) in her history, I belatedly recognize why my friend was upset. But I admit that I, too, was blinded by the illusion that power, military power, could force peace. So I have seen Americans burn and destroy a village "in order to save it."

We have all heard historian Lord Acton's "Power corrupts — absolute power corrupts absolutely." When will we begin to believe what we know from vast, tragic experience? It is demonic to think that power will yield results. Yet when America's impoverished minorities rise in protest, Congress immediately votes funds for additional police and equipment but spends months, even years, before doing anything about easing the conditions of the undereducated and underemployed.

We are still believing the demonic old lie. "Then the Devil took him up and showed him in a second all the kingdoms of the world. 'I will give you all this power, and all this wealth,' the Devil told him. 'It was all handed over to me and I can give it to anyone I choose'" (Luke 4:5-6, TEV).

There are plenty of times when the Devil's arrogant claims sound true enough. "It has been put in my hands, and I can give it to anyone I choose," he boasts. Watching Stalin operate in Russia made one almost believe Satan. The Russian dictator always feared and hated the Germans, but he overcame this dread in order to sign a pact with Hitler since Russia gained considerable territory with apparently little effort out of the treacherous deal. Then when Hitler attacked Russia, Stalin's hatred knew no bounds. Many Russian soldiers and much land were lost to the advancing Germans when they first attacked. Years later, when the Russians regained this territory, they also released their surviving comrades from the German prisoner-of-war camps. So sick was Stalin's suspicion of the Germans, that every Russian soldier imprisoned by the Nazis was now considered dangerous to his homeland. So the captive Russians never were actually released. Their homeward-bound trains, which at first promised freedom, actually became new prisons taking them off to their new detention camps. In *A Day in the Life of Ivan Denisovich,* Alexander Solzhenitsyn describes this tragedy in Siberia, which almost seems to justify the Devil's extravagant pretensions. There certainly seem to be enough people who behave as though life really is a jungle and the only ruler is Beelzebub.

Against this dying tradition that the big boss is the "Lord of the Flies," Jesus asserted a claim for the Lord of Life. Jesus responded to Satan: "Worship the Lord your God and serve only him!" (Luke 4:8, TEV).

Again Jesus resorted to Deuteronomy. Israel had been instructed what they were to do when they were settled in the promised land: "When you eat your fill there, be careful not to forget the Lord who brought you out of Egypt, out of the land of slavery. You shall fear the Lord your God, serve him alone and take your oaths in his name" (Deuteronomy 6:12-13, NEB). For Jesus these were not just words spoken in some ancient time but were actually spoken for his time and his condition. So he readily replied to the second temptation: "Worship the Lord your God and serve only him!" (Luke 4:8, TEV).

Jesus was well aware of the entire passage. In our texts, the next verses read: "You must not follow other gods, gods of the nations around you; if you do, the Lord your God who is in your midst will be angry with you, and he will sweep you away off the face of the earth, for the Lord your God is a jealous god" (Deuteronomy 6:14-15, NEB).

Professor Robert Bellah in his scholarly article entitled "Civil Religion in America" has traced the idea of the United States as the new Israel.[1] This motif has energized many American patriots and statesmen. The tyrants from whom the Pilgrims fled are associated with old Pharaoh and Egypt. Their perilous crossing of the Atlantic is identified with the miraculous crossing of the Red Sea. The new America became the promised land to the religiously minded settlers. Professor Bellah has been able to show historically how this cluster of ideas has influenced American politics, literature, and culture in general. As this democratic nation celebrates its two hundredth anniversary, men well may reflect upon what God's jealousy means.

The Hebrew prophets interpreted the jealous character of God to mean that he watched intently over the affairs of his people, keeping especially a watchful eye on the conditions of orphans and widows. The prophets understood God's jeal-

[1] Cf. Robert Bellah, "Civil Religion in America," *Daedalus*, Journal of the American Academy of Arts and Sciences, Winter, 1967, pp. 1-21.

14

ousy to mean that God had a driving desire for mercy and justice.

Any modern nation, but especially one whose national leadership year in and year out calls upon divine guidance, must recognize that its future is being written in the treatment being accorded to the innocent and unprotected within present society. Any nation that writes tax laws and relief measures to benefit those in power can expect difficult times in the future. Whether it be China in the nineteenth century or France in the eighteenth, the government of the favored few is bound to come upon difficult times.

Hosea declared:

Therefore have I lashed you through the prophets
and torn you to shreds with my words;
loyalty is my desire, not sacrifice,
not whole-offerings but the knowledge of God.

Hosea 6:5-6, NEB

Such loyalty is far more than just a religious commitment. It involves a social zeal. The true worshiper is not the one who donates the offering at the temple but the man who sees to it that justice is enacted in the streets. God's prophet declares that trouble brews when a nation's leaders exploit their positions for their own benefit. A society run by the few in order to exploit the many is certain to attract God's jealous anger.

What of the nation that depends upon its own power to make its way in the world? Israel was denounced by the prophet:

Because you have trusted in your chariots,
in the number of your warriors,
the tumult of war shall arise against your people,
and all your fortresses shall be razed. . . .

Hosea 10:13-14, NEB

Whether the nation is Old Israel or the New Israel born across the seas, God as ruler of history is just and holds all men accountable. This was the magnificent tradition upon which Jesus drew as he contested with the ruler of darkness.

In response to such demonic braggadocio, which vaunted, "It was all handed over to me and I can give it to anyone I choose" (Luke 4:6, TEV), Jesus responds affirmatively: "Worship the Lord your God and serve only him!" (Luke 4:8, TEV).

Having successfully mastered two of the diabolical shortcuts for bringing in God's reign, Jesus still had to wrestle with another cunningly contrived test, the temptation of trying

15

for miracles and testing God. "Then the Devil took him to Jerusalem and set him on the highest point of the Temple, and said to him, 'If you are God's Son, throw yourself down from here'" (Luke 4:9, TEV). Now such a crude invitation did not become the Devil. He used Scripture to urge that Jesus use spectacular showmanship in order to attract an instant following. How many modern leaders fall for this pitch, without the scriptural wrappings! Men make grandiose promises just to grab a headline. Celebrities spend extravagantly in order to keep the fans interested. To gain the attention of people is not easy, and some are tempted to use any means to get their message heard.

But Jesus knew that this practice was more than a question of exploiting the gullible nature of people. More serious was the fact that God would be put to the test if Jesus tried to carry out such a stupid stunt. As William Barclay put it: ". . . there is no good in putting yourself deliberately into a threatening situation . . . and then expecting God to rescue you from it." [2]

I am not certain that I have ever been privileged to hear a sermon preached on the text of Jesus' reply: "You must not put the Lord your God to the test" (Luke 4:12, TEV). This verse does not seem to be very much in the consciousness of modern man. Certainly the way most of us drive our automobiles would indicate that a Christian has an inalienable right to test God, not to speak of testing the other drivers, as well as his own passengers.

About a decade ago something that passed for American foreign policy was called "brinkmanship." Perhaps if a few more state department officials had been exposed to some sermons on this text, they might have reexamined their approach. It is never too late to reflect upon this verse.

All too many families today test their own nerve endings, their banker's credulity, and perhaps even the Almighty in how they handle family finances. Actually how many marriages finally do break apart because the couple refused to be responsible about living appropriately within their income? To ask God to bless their union and then to flirt constantly with bankruptcy is straining their covenant relationship, if not actually testing God.

[2] William Barclay, ed., *The Gospel of Matthew* (Philadelphia: The Westminster Press, 1959), vol. 1, p. 63.

Jesus again drew upon his knowledge of Deuteronomy: "You must not challenge the Lord your God as you challenged him at Massah" (Deuteronomy 6:16, NEB). The word "Massah" means challenge. The event which prompted Moses to name the place Massah is described in Exodus. When the tired Israelites came to a camp in the desert which was without water, the people began to protest.

> When they said, "Give us water to drink," Moses said, "why do you dispute with me? Why do you challenge the Lord?" There the people became so thirsty that they raised an outcry against Moses: "Why have you brought us out of Egypt with our children and our herds to let us all die of thirst?" (Exodus 17:2-3, NEB).

Moses pushed the panic button and, fearing for his own safety, called upon God for help and advice. God instructed him how to give the people the water they needed. The account in Exodus concludes with Moses naming the place Massah (challenge) and Meribah (Dispute) "because the Israelites had disputed with him and challenged the Lord with their question, 'Is the Lord in our midst or not?'" (Exodus 17:7, NEB).

There was no question of God's presence in Jesus' experience. The blessing which followed the act of baptism was proof indeed of God's watchful interest. Jesus shared the prophetic vision which saw God taking care of the widow in her solitude, the orphan in his need. Such a providing God was well aware of the human situation. Jesus' eyes were wide open to the heavenly Father's merciful activities among men.

So Jesus rejected Satan's test: "to do big things, boy, you've got to get the attention of the crowd. You won't get hurt if you are who you say you are." Jesus' response was: "You are not to put the Lord your God to the test" (Luke 4:12, TEV).

The lessons Jesus learned in these dark hours actually shaped the course of his life. He would again be tempted in increasingly more subtle ways. In time, political cliques and religious groups would put him to the test. Even his closest friends, his disciples, would sometimes tempt him to deviate from the stern task, and he would fight the impulse: "Away with you, Satan" (Matthew 16:23, NEB).

But as a result of this time of temptation, the main outlines of his mission had been worked out. He would avoid the way of winning popularity by buying up some followers; he would not resort to violence and force to bring in God's new regime. He would have nothing to do with the religious wonder-workers who by spectacular feats attracted followers. The task he chose for himself was the most difficult one. Without any detailed master plan, but only with his confidence in God's leading, he would move out and each day seek to obey the directing spirit of the loving Father. Nothing very spectacular, hardly instant success, but each day a single step forward. Where he could recognize signs of God's dawning kingdom, he would call attention to it. Where he could take part in God's movement of liberation, he would get right into the action. He would try to gather a small group of students to share his pilgrimage and perhaps, later, expand the circle. But always he must trust in God's guidance and obey the promptings he sensed.

Luke concludes this critical episode in Jesus' life with these words: "So, having come to the end of all his temptations, the devil departed, biding his time" (Luke 4:13, NEB). Jesus' entire career was an ongoing conflict with the powers of darkness. The climax of this life and death struggle was the crucifixion post on the awful Friday. The loss inflicted by hate, suspicion, and death was resolved only by God's intervention. The total defeat of the cross was turned into victory through the resurrection. These events were yet a lifetime away when Jesus first wrestled with the basic form of his ministry. Having made these fundamental decisions, he was ready to undertake his mission.

2. WHEN HIS HOMETOWN TRIED TO LYNCH HIM
Luke 4:16-30; Mark 6:2-6

Jesus faced a severe crisis at the beginning of his career, when his hometown rose up against him. Trying to understand why his own neighbors and old acquaintances tried to lynch him may provide insight into our present religious situation. What are the dangers of trying to silence the prophetic voice? We will attempt to answer the question:

Early in his ministry, Jesus attended the sabbath worship in his hometown synagogue. Seeing the youthful teacher in their midst, the elders invited him to read and interpret the prophets. Jesus read from Isaiah 61.

As best we know, Jesus was brought up in this very congregation. This is where he had acquired his intimate knowledge of the Scriptures. Among those who heard him speak on that sabbath were the men who had instructed him in the Law, the prophets, and the writings. Scripture reading was what the synagogue was all about. It was here that the faithful gathered in order to study God's Word. Why, then, did these men who had watched Jesus grow in his knowledge of the scriptures run him out of town and attempt to throw him over the cliff?

This crisis, faced by Jesus early in his prophetic ministry, throws light upon three facets of our contemporary religious situation. First, God's liberating and therefore revolutionary activity is often seen by religious persons as past event; second, the prophetic element often remains unrecognized; and third, we prefer that the dynamic and prophetic voices go away and leave us alone.

Jesus read the prophets dynamically: "It is beginning right here, right now." His listeners heard the prophets passively: "It happened a long time ago." The very instructors who had helped Jesus develop his knowledge and love of the Hebrew Scriptures were content to let the prophets stand as testimonials of the past.

Jesus saw the prophets as present-day witnesses. He responded to the Scriptures more actively than his own teachers. He studied the sacred writings and expected to see God's work *jump into action!*

He experienced God's Word as *kinetic energy:*

People are changed,
  societies are being transformed,
    history is being made
because God is filling full the destructive and constructive power of his Word, right now and right here.

Jesus returned to his hometown and taught his own teachers that "God's Word is breaking in upon your lives, upon this community, upon your affairs this very day — in our time, in our place!"

The problem to which Jesus addressed himself is our problem as well. We tend to teach the Bible as something that happened back there. We seem to say, "In those days. . . ." Reflecting on the long ago past soon begins to sound like: "Once upon a time. . . ." Nothing contributes as much yawning space to the generation gap as the fact that we, who represent a senior and more conservative generation, seem to be putting all events in the *past* tense.

Many in the present youthful generation insist on putting events in the *present* tense.

For example, many in the parental generation associate the word "revolution" with something that took place in the past, specifically, the American Revolution of 1776. The offspring generation sees the event of revolution as present, NOW. *Today* we are caught up in an escalating revolution which is radically changing the social, economic, and political shapes of our society.

Or again, many of our political leaders who are now in their fifties, sixties, or seventies see justice and liberty as something that was accomplished in the past. This is why, for example, middle America seems to want "strict constructionists" on the Supreme Court. Justice is understood to be some event that took place back there. Liberty is something realized in the past. For the militant young, justice and liberty are something to be gained in the present; so they must be fought for in the here and now.

In recent years, the American judicial system has been subjected to great stresses. From one side come the pressures for rigid interpretation and severe penalties. From the other extreme come boisterous behavior in the courtroom and even physical assault on the judges. One of the earlier such cases was the trial of the Chicago Seven. These seven men were militant figures arrested during the demonstrations connected with the 1968 Chicago Democratic Party Convention. Even the law they were accused of violating was itself a strain on the constitutional and judicial process, for a Congress, dominated by elderly men, had passed a law which many young militants saw as an attempt to curb their civil liberties of public assembly and free speech.

The trial of the Chicago Seven is difficult to assess. As the septuagenarian federal judge tried to *interpret* law, he depended on traditions which have come down to us over the centuries. The militants who stood before him were not interested in the interpreting of law but in the making of history. I myself take gravely the implications of the Chicago trials and feel that both the judge and the accused have injured a very fragile instrument, namely our judicial system. But no matter how any of us may feel about the case, we all are painfully aware of the response which many young persons in America made to the contempt sentences handed out by the angry judge. The militant youth of America spilled out into the streets of our cities and attacked federal buildings and even burned a bank. While such mob action deserves condemnation, our expressions of outrage should not blind us to what is happening. Young people are marching against what they sense are injustices.

We in our churches are as ill equipped as were the religious leaders of Nazareth to appreciate what God's Word is bringing into being in our present day. Jesus said to his own people, "Today in your very hearing this text has come true." We need to ask of ourselves: "Where, in today's world, is good news being announced to the poor? From where is release coming to the captives? From whence comes the recovery of sight for the emotionally, physically, and spiritually blind? What forces are at work in our world to let the broken victims go free?"

The first dilemma with which Jesus' experience in his hometown acquaints us is this: if our religion is something that has to do only with a dead past, and if our faith is only pious ritual without any active sharing in God's action in today's world, then we will miss the present saving activity of God. In allowing our faith to be past and passive, we are missing out on the action. If we see God's Word only as something that happened back in Bible times, we lack the liberating quality of authentic faith.

The second matter in Jesus' experience that contributes to better appreciation of our modern Christian dilemma is expressed in Jesus' words, "No prophet is recognized in his own country."

21

Whenever a prophetic spirit emerges in our midst, we find that person interpreting God's ways in terms of the everyday. Jeremiah spoke of broken pots and empty water reservoirs; Hosea spoke of persistent lovers and unfaithful wives; Amos spoke of the house builder's plumb line; Jesus told of the housewife at her chores and the farmer in his fields.

Even as we listen to the prophetic voice, the danger awaits us; we are so ready to say, "Why, nobody knows the objects we use everyday better than we do."

So while the prophetic voice declares to us, "The commonplace reveals the eternal," we listen with deaf ears. We ignore ultimate reality because we have become accustomed to accepting the ever present reality.

We are so accustomed to what is common,
 so much at home with the familiar,
so matter of fact about every day,
 that we miss out on the prophetic element possible in any particular event, encounter, or personality.

What is the harm in ignoring the prophetic element in our human history? The failure to recognize the prophet is fatal to men and societies.

Because we ignore the prophets,
we become so afraid of death that we are unable to confront life;
we are so anxious to avoid turbulence that we are incapable of building stability;
we become so obsessed with
 possessing inert objects *of* matter
that we miss out on enjoying living subjects *that* matter.

The history of mankind records the emergence of various prophetic personalities and movements. Some have helped the people weather a crisis or face a new era. History also tells of nations who rejected the prophet.

The Hebrews followed Moses. Athens put Socrates to death. Industrial England responded to the prophetic urgings of Wesley and Wilberforce. English society has since gone through evolution. Czarist Russia imprisoned every prophetic spirit, and violent revolution resulted.

In the history of these United States the Union rallied behind the prophetic leadership of Abraham Lincoln. In more recent times the pages of history are more obscure. We continue to have prophetic spirits. There was the man who was imprisoned in the Birmingham jail, and there was the man who telephoned Birmingham and who also sat down with César Chávez. But both Martin Luther King and Robert Kennedy belong among the prophets who have been killed in our time, and the modern list keeps growing. Lest there be any misunderstanding, let no one think that what I am saying is, "Hey, look at me; I am a prophet." No, indeed. What I am trying to say is, "Hey, look all around you. There are prophets in our midst. Let's pay attention to them. If we listen, perhaps we will survive as a people. If we continue to allow the prophetic spirits to be shot at and imprisoned, then surely we will perish as a nation."

The common meal around which Christians gather, called the Lord's Table, is one such prophetic sign set in the very midst of our ordinary life. Where do you and I see the broken body and the spilled-out life of Christ in what is happening all about us?

I see it in teenagers who care much — and whose parents seem to care less. I see it in our barber shops and beauty parlors where — snip, snip — a little hair is cut; snip, snip, a personality is chopped down. I see it in the brave soul who dares to speak up and ask, when a vicious rumor is recounted at one of our coffee klatches, "Are you sure? Have you checked your source? Are we aware of what we are saying and doing to that person by our gossip?"

Where do we find the brokenness? Where do we find the healing word? Who needs the reconciling touch? Who is the person willing to risk in order to allow reconciliation?

We who live in America's beautiful small towns and comfortable suburbs especially have much to learn. I don't think I have ever lived anywhere that reminds me more of what Jesus' Nazareth must have been like than my present small town does. We have a beautiful community richly blessed by God. We are a religious people with church members active in practically every enterprise and organization. Yet we have the most difficult time giving people recognition, acceptance, and credibility. I myself am acquainted with persons, past and present, in this town who have gained worthy reputations, some with enviable international reputations; yet they have never been honored in their own hometown.

If we fail to recognize the giants among us, how can we appreciate the lesser figures, but no lesser prophetic spirits, in

23

our midst? I think of our young people. The prophetic element is alive in today's youth.

The prophetic spirit animates the discussion of the environment. College students have led the way in arousing the concern for ecology. Tom Wicker of the *New York Times* once spoke to Oregon Republicans and told them that

the environment is probably the most important issue of our times, but "too many politicians see it as a convenient issue. . . ."

He noted that many of these politicians are those "who were cutting down the redwoods" yesterday but now find livability more popular than taxes and schools.

Wicker said the problem of environment . . . cannot be challenged without meeting the accompanying urban problems of mass transportation, improving the cities, and facing the vast number of social problems.[1]

Perhaps the reason we ignore the prophetic element in our own history is that prophetic spirits make us uncomfortable. They want us to change, to reform, to do something other than what we are already doing. This is the third factor in our modern Christian dilemma.

Now if Jesus really wanted the approval of his old synagogue school teachers, why didn't he just give them that old-time religion? Why mess with questions of the economy; why should the poor hear good news? Why meddle with the power structure? If folks were in jail, they deserved to be there; and to talk about releasing captives was to stir up false hopes. Why interfere with the establishment? Who was Jesus blaming for causing broken victims? If he didn't love Galilee, why didn't he leave it?

By now you have figured out the end of the story. Yes, Jesus lost his audience. They just were not prepared for his message. They had tried their best to bring him up as a good religious boy, but somewhere he had gotten these strange notions, these awful ideas. Who knows where the young people get some of their ideas these days?

Jesus' remarks made those at the synagogue angry. How dare he say such things! After all they had done for him. They were angry, bitter, violent!

The whole congregation was furious. They jumped up, ran him out of town, and were all set to throw him over a cliff.

Then Luke tells us, "But he walked straight through them all, and went away."

[1] Doug Yocom, " 'Faddish' Environment Concern Slammed," *Oregon Journal,* February 28, 1970.

24

One thing about the prophetic element in life — if you just ignore it, it will go away. You have to put up with it for a while; but if you don't let it get you, the prophetic will go away. And what's left after the prophetic has gone away? Things go back as they were. Things go along just as they have always gone along. The wheeler-dealers continue to wheel and deal — for a while.

What have we lost when in our fury we drive the prophetic from our midst?

Maybe some of the poor among us miss out on a little good news — but then the poor are used to missing out on the good things of life;

and the prisoners soon get used to their prison house and their imprisoned lives;

and the blind remain without sight; victims are broken with no one to heal them and make them whole.

What do we miss when we silence the voice of the prophet?

Not too much, unless it is God's spokesman.

What do we miss when we get rid of the prophet?

Not very much, unless it is an awareness of God's activity.

What do we miss?

Not much, unless it is God.

3. ACCUSED OF AN UNCONVENTIONAL MINISTRY
Mark 1:21-28; 2:18-28

Early in Mark's description of Jesus' ministry, the reader is made aware that Jesus did not follow a conventional pattern. He did not teach the way the other religious leaders taught. His disciples did not behave the way the disciples of other teachers behaved. Jesus interpreted the powerful action of God quite differently from the orthodox religious interpretations of how God worked.

We live in a day marked by a great variety of ministries. All claim to be authentic modes of Christian servanthood. A closer study of Jesus' own unconventional ministry should help us develop more effective forms of service.

Three questions in the first two chapters of Mark's Gospel deserve examination. They focus upon the response of Jesus' co-religionists to his unconventional style. These questions are: Why is it that John's disciples and the disciples of the Pharisees are fasting, but yours are not? Who gave you this authority? What have you to do with us? (Mark 2:18; 11:28; cf. 1:27; 1-24).

The first inquiry concerns the different approach evident in the practices of Jesus and his closest associates. Jesus was accused of not conforming to expected practices of piety. "Why is it that the disciples of John the Baptist and the disciples of the Pharisees fast, but yours do not?" (Mark 2:18, TEV). Considering there are many conventional ways of practicing religion, Jesus' critics queried: Why does *your* way have to be so different?

In Luke 13, we read of a woman who had been crippled for eighteen years and whom Jesus healed on the sabbath. His accusers continued, "Look, why are they doing what is forbidden on the Sabbath?" (Mark 2:24, NEB).

Why did Jesus undertake an unconventional ministry? One reason may have been his awareness of God's activity which runs contrary to popular expectations. Much of religious custom and practice seems to limit God's presence to special practices in certain times and certain places. Jesus knew that God really makes himself known in unusual ways, unexpected events, and secular situations.

Throughout his ministry, Jesus emphasized the surprising means and strange places wherein God demonstrates his pres-

26

ence. Jesus called our attention to God's active work in children and mustard trees, in flying birds and flowering meadow, in widows and offering plates, in publicans confessing their sins, and in streetwalkers who demonstrated concern. God uses the impoverished and the socially outcast to express his divine purpose.

Jesus himself sometimes treated established religious customs so casually that he aroused rebuke from the pious. Luke recalls: "The Pharisee noticed with surprise that he [Jesus] had not begun by washing before the meal" (Luke 11:37, NEB).

Why would Jesus flaunt ordinary Jewish religious practice? Perhaps because he was aware that certain religious customs, though they appear to be trivial, keep many persons from practicing the religious life. The strict caste of the Pharisees, well-meaning though it was, actually created the social class of Am haarez, the people of the land. These were the outcasts of Israel. They constituted large numbers of persons who were unable to fulfill the exacting demands of the religious law.

As we study religious history, many such instances can be found. A happier chapter is provided by the beginnings of the modern Methodist Church. John Wesley was a priest of the established Church of England. He became painfully aware of the inadequacy of his church's ministry to the growing mass of workers created by the industrial revolution. Religious services were restricted to church buildings located in traditional parishes, which now were far from the new industrial centers. John Wesley's burning concern was how to provide a ministry to these working men. Even he, however, was initially shocked by George Whitfield's unconventional resolution of the problem. Whitfield preached outdoors in open fields, which were near enough to the industrial towns that the workmen could readily gather there. Convinced after taking part in such open air meetings, Wesley adopted this unconventional ministry. To this flexibility, England and America owe the presence of the lively working classes among our churches.

Today, what new unconventional ministries await us? Where do we find the persons whose lives are relatively untouched by the liberating word of God's love? What have changing conditions been doing to the way people make use of their time? Where are the new places where people today gather?

In recent months I have been studying many different ages in the history of Western man. I am impressed that time and

27

again, Christ-filled men and women have discovered appropriate means of responding to the challenges which come with each new age. At one time it was the monastic movement. At another time it was the creation of universities. And still another time the means of response was a radical transformation of all institutions.

This closer study of man's history encourages one to look about and examine the many unconventional forms of ministry now offered. I am hopeful that appropriate forms of serving are emerging. It may be among the Glenmary Sisters of the Catholic Church, who stretch their ministries from the Appalachian hills to the northern cities, for it is these highways that the poor follow in their search for life and work. The Glenmary Sisters work in the rural areas of America's eastern mountain range. Their ministries have been molded along the pattern of the people whom they serve. In "good times," which means when jobs are available, the mountain people move to the industrial cities "up north." In bad times, called "recession" by far-removed economists, the unemployable families drift back to their little plots of ground carved out of the mountainsides. These Catholic nuns provide a moving mission to these persons in their need.

The signs of renewal may be seen in the various communes of the countryside or the committed communities that gather in the urban centers. Baptist home missionaries have pioneered in a ministry to high-rise apartments. They seek to discover whether Christian "management" of housing projects can provide a more wholesome influence. Can newcomers to the city be helped? Can broken families find support? Can young persons be encouraged to continue their schooling and find suitable employment? The style of missionary efforts changes to meet the new demands of society increasingly shaped by the pressures of technology. Both at home and abroad, Christian missionaries seek new ways to serve.

The second question, "Who gave you this authority?" was asked of Jesus by the priests who served in the temple and by the lawyers who interpreted the traditional code as well as by the elders who governed the religious community. Their questions provide evidence of the fact that Jesus scandalized the orthodox leaders of his day.

The most religious of men were not prepared then for his coming, nor are we now. For the experience of God is not

28

always what men have come to associate with a "religious experience." As true today as it was in Jesus' time, what men often call "the religious experience" is not always an experiencing of God.

To meet neatly spelled out conditions of membership is easier apparently than to fulfill the moral obligations of true piety. Jesus accused the religionists, "You clean the outside of cup and plate . . . but have no care for justice and the love of God" (Luke 11:39, 42, NEB). Can we sense the similarity of his accusation to the criticisms made of our culture and our nation?

Just as we have difficulty replying to the criticisms of how we run "our establishment," so the elders of Judea had trouble responding to Jesus' criticism of the religious establishment. Their clumsy rejoinder was an attempted attack upon his prerogative, for Jesus did teach and behave as one who had authority. This meant that he spoke and acted as did the prophets of the Old Testament, under the direct authorization of God.

Jesus did not depend upon the past for his authority. Even today we turn to recent and ancient learned men to lend authority to our teaching. Halford Luccock comments that Jesus "did not live in the prison house of quotation marks."[1] This freedom from tradition identifies Jesus' strength. Unlike the religious leaders of his day, and of our own day, Jesus found his sources of sovereignty in the direct application of God-given insights to the problems of his day.

However, let's not be too harsh on those of us who find ourselves confined by "quotation marks." As were the scribes, who interpreted the legal code to Jesus' generation, so modern scholars are forced to draw up precedents to justify their arguments. What is modern man's reliance upon "the old-time religion" but this yearning to stay with the old? Thus, as modern churchmen, we are as offended as were the scribes and Pharisees. We either ignore or hide the offensiveness of much of Jesus' teachings by pretending that it is impractical for our day. Do we seriously believe that the earth belongs to the meek? Not if the aggressiveness we teach our children is any indication of our true stance: "Don't let him take that away from you! Don't let them get away with THAT!" Such

[1] Halford Luccock, *Interpreter's Bible*, ed. George A. Buttrick (Nashville: Abingdon Press, 1954), vol. 7, p. 660.

commonsense responses indicate that modern-day Christians certainly are affronted by Jesus' teaching. How many Christians can really accept Jesus' straightforward teaching that "those who work for peace among men" are happy! Whether in Germany or the United States, the most righteous of the war makers have come from Christian congregations. Of course when I went to war, the purpose was to "win the peace." But if Jesus really meant that "those who work for peace among men" are happy, I was wrong in believing, along with my generation, that peace is gained by waging war. Then I suppose I do find *that* teaching of Jesus somewhat offensive — or at least, unrealistic.

As we read this account of Jesus' dealing with the Pharisees, it is easy to find ourselves on the side of Jesus and saying: "How come, Mr. and Mrs. Pharisee, you are such dumb bunnies? Can't you see what this wonderful teacher, Jesus, is getting at? Can't you understand that just going to the same old 'religious' place and doing the usual 'religious' routine does not allow the wonderful power of God to take hold and operate in your life?"

It is easy to get inside this event. We readily identify ourselves on the side of Jesus, and we feel pity for the Pharisees. This attitude is our "religious" way of avoiding the pointed teachings of Jesus.

Actually, the Pharisees were awfully good people. They were far better at this *doing* of religion than we, their modern counterparts, are. They were diligent, consistent, and knowledgeable. They worked hard at what they believed in. They worked regularly at it, and they knew well the many complicated regulations which governed their religious life. None of this can be said for many of us. We seem to work in spurts at being religious. We are not very consistent in our zeal. (In historic fact, the very institution of the revival as a characteristic phenomenon of American religious expression would seem to indicate that we are rather irregular in our religious devotion.) Certainly, most of us know terribly little about religion. As one who tries to teach religion to college students, I think I can document that statement with ample evidence.

Are we sufficiently surprised at what Jesus has to say to us? Have we so covered over the radical demands which Jesus made upon people that we miss the surprising note in his challenges to us? Are his teachings so familiar to us, and do we take his commandments so much for granted, that we are no longer amazed by his teachings?

The third question which was asked of Jesus was "What have you to do with us?" (Mark 1:24). The demoniac recognized Jesus as a teacher who could banish the demon that possessed him. "Are you here to destroy us?" (1:24, TEV).

Sometimes it is *evil* which must acknowledge the presence of good. When good people ignore reality, sometimes the evil among us recognize the presence of the holy.

Mark makes plain that while the religious leaders were demanding that Jesus show his credentials, the demon possessed was the one who recognized his presence. "I know who you are," the man possessed of an evil spirit shouted, "You are God's holy messenger!" (Mark 1:24, TEV).

When persons who were dominated by evil forces could recognize the source of Jesus' power and authority, why did the religious people fail to identify the Holy One of God?

Exorcism describes the experience by which an authoritative word of command expels a demon from a troubled person. Many people in Jesus' time thought that being personally possessed by demonic powers caused various kinds of mental or even physical illness. But such madness or paralysis, whether primitively described or modernly analyzed, does not mean that the individual sufferer has deliberately gone over to evil, though sometimes this may be the case.

More often, the evil has infected the whole human society, disrupting family life, falsifying human relationships, and thrusting tensions upon personal associations.

Perhaps we live in such evil times. Normally healthy relationships, such as the family, are seriously questioned. A college student sometimes feels that something is wrong if he or she happens to have a wholesome and happy relationship with his mother, father, brothers, and sisters.

Are husband and wife to enjoy each other and find personal satisfaction and sexual fulfillment within the bonds of marriage? Not according to all the films which regularly play the "neighborhood theaters." Not faithfulness but infidelity seems to be the theme of modern novelists.

Yet our human experiences would indicate that happiness is more likely to occur where two persons make a commitment to each other's well-being. Such a vow to will the good of the other involves one's fidelity to the other. In the *freedom* of such faithful devotion, we are able to discover our true personalities. Deep relationships can grow only in a trusting relationship. This certainly is the evidence I have found in two decades of personal and family counseling.

When will the writers of fiction catch up with the facts of life? Only in the atmosphere of trust does the true personhood enjoy liberty enough to emerge. Only in faithful relationships can true union come into being. Especially in our personal lives and our family concerns, we must be surprised by Jesus' insights:

we live in faithful relationship *not* because it is the law;

we live in a trusting communion not because we are *required* to do so;

we live in honest and open communication not because we *ought* to,

because trust, faith, and openness cannot be decreed.

Rather, we allow the surprises of God to overtake us in the normal, everyday dealings with others because we have committed ourselves to *doing the good* toward the other. In dealing justly, in conferring mercy, in showing forgiveness, God is able to work his miracles of justice, mercy, and loving-kindness in our lives.

This is not the righteousness of the "uptight." This is not the well-doing of those who must do it "just right." This is a miracle that comes because God has been able to move through us and about us. Our lives grow out of our promises freely given to one another, to look out for the good of the other person. When we honestly try to serve our fellow, we are often surprised to find God serving with us.

We have considered three questions which outline the unconventional character of Jesus' ministry.

Why are your disciples behaving differently?

Who gave you this authority?

What have you to do with us?

It is possible for us to handle the first question intellectually. One may compare the models of ministry. Let's see the legalistic model of the Pharisees as compared with the Prophets. How about the model of John the Baptist? Is it better than the model of Jesus?

We can even keep the second question at a distance. "By what authority?" we ask of Jesus. By what right does the church tell me what to do? By what sanction does our society dictate to us? What makes parents think they can dictate to . . .? These arguments are all intended to keep us from becoming involved.

In asking such questions, we are trying to put off the real challenges:

What is my responsibility to my fellowman?

What might I be doing to better the relationship?

How can I contribute to improving the situation?

How can I be a part of the healing and growing process?

The third question cannot be handled abstractly or intellectually. It cannot be put off and kept at bay. The third question is intensely personal and agonizing, for it involves us. To ask, "What have you to do with us?" immediately brings out the personal question, "Jesus, what have I to do with you?" When we openly try to grapple with that question, we may find a deepening awareness of the real authority of Jesus.

4. WHEN HIS MOTHER AND BROTHERS TRIED TO PUT HIM AWAY
Mark 3:20-35

The home shapes the human person. In today's world many families are having difficulty managing to avoid two equal dangers related to human growth. Too little care and uneven guidance produce a less than stable personality. Too close attention and too rigid direction may smother the individual capacity to become a distinctive personality.

Let us examine one crisis in the life of Jesus to see what light may be shed upon this important relationship between family and personality. In the study of this turning point in Jesus' personal history we will inquire into three major questions:

Why was his family so concerned about Jesus?

Why was Jesus forced to reject their solution to his problem?

What was the result of this critical juncture in Jesus' own family situation?

Thus we will begin with the intimate family circle, proceed to the broken family circle, and then move to the greater family circle.

The first question in the study of this crisis in Jesus' life is: Why was his family upset? The Gospel of Mark records: "When his family heard of this, they set out to take charge of him; for people were saying that he was out of his mind" (Mark 3:21, NEB). It appears that as soon as they heard rumors that their eldest son and brother was in trouble, the mother and brothers set out to do something about it. In a word, his family cared.

We know little about the personal family of Jesus, but what little historical evidence we do have provides every indication of close family ties. We read of Mary's visiting and staying with her cousin Elizabeth. We can read of Joseph's loving concern for his betrothed. In Luke's account of the circumcision we recognize the piety and practice of a typical family in Judaism. We see the couple a decade richer in human experience responding good-naturedly when their pre-teen son gets so involved with serious talk in the temple that he forgets to let them know of his whereabouts.

Perhaps we need no greater evidence of Christ's humanity than Luke's record of his losing track of time. Any parent will recognize this, for we hear it frequently as the adolescent honestly says, "But I didn't know what the time was." There is also a human note as John's Gospel portrays the mother and her firstborn son attending a Jewish wedding.

Although there is no diary-like account of the domestic life in the home of Mary and Joseph, we do have every indication that they were a caring family. Mark wrote, "When his family heard of this, they set out to take charge of him" (Mark 3:21, NEB). His family recognized their responsibility in helping their brother in his personal development. They shared a concern for him.

There was for a while a popular saying, "The family that prays together, stays together." Without detracting from the value which this saying has had for many a Christian home, let's expand it and perhaps update it a little:

The kind of praying that does the family the most good, indeed, the only kind of praying that does anybody good, is the praying that rises out of caring. The family that cares together is a family prepared to pray together.

And why care? Why pray? Merely to *stay* together? In today's "moving-about" world? We care for one another, and we pray with and for each other in order to equip each member of the family to go out into this topsy-turvy world.

The mother and brothers of Jesus *cared* for him, *prayed* for him, and went out to take charge of him.

Now we come to the second part of the problem. We noted, in the first place, that the family has the important responsibility of helping the growing personality come into its being. We shall explore next an equally important factor — the necessity for the individual person to do his own deciding and his own growing, in order to be himself.

We seem to find conflicting clues in this short passage from Mark. The story states that in the popular opinion of the common masses, Jesus was a great prophet. ". . . such a crowd collected round them that they had no chance to eat" (Mark 3:20, NEB). Jesus' family held their own opinions on such proceedings.

Mark's account, in the sixth chapter, of Jesus' visit to Nazareth is silent as to the views of Jesus' family. But the very way in which the hometowners reacted says a great deal. "What wisdom is this that has been given him? . . . Isn't he the carpenter, the son of Mary, and the brother of James, Joses,

Judas, and Simon? Aren't his sisters living here?" (Mark 6:3, TEV). In this way, Nazareth rejected him. It would have been hard for Mary and her family not to have been influenced by their neighbors. After all, they had to live with these people day after day. And Jesus had been gone for a long time.

"The reports we hear, the people he is now associating with, the accusations against him! There are certain unsavory characters among his disciples. Simon, everyone knows, is a militant. There is Matthew, a former tax gatherer. What are his connections with the Roman overlords, I wonder? What did he do with all of his ill-gained wealth, huh? You know that Jesus actually allows women to travel with him. Some of their reputations would make any mother worry."

According to Mark's Gospel, the family of Jesus never did accept him during his lifetime. They seem to have considered as madness his leaving the comfort and security of Nazareth. Why did he give up his father's trade? Why did he turn his back upon a settled life? Why was he mixed up with such odd situations and such a mixed bag of associates?

As a family devoted to orthodox Jewish piety, Mary and her sons had cause for concern. They early learned that Jesus was teaching doctrine that was independent of established teaching. Then they heard that he was actually opposing the scribal authorities. They had some reason to suspect his sanity. So they tried to rescue him.

Jesus was rooted in the depths of Judaism's history. Yet Jesus was one who transcended history. This important struggle allows us to see how one person moved from the historical condition to the transcendent principle.

Why did Jesus reject his family's solution for his difficulties? So far, we have been looking at Jesus' family problem from the family's point of view. What was Jesus' situation when they found him?

His family arrived in time to find Jesus involved in a serious conflict with the religious authorities. The outcome of this controversy was crucial if he was to carry out his intended mission. From Jerusalem there had come some doctors of the Law. They accused him of being in league with the prince of devils. If they could prove this accusation, they could convict him of blasphemy. The maximum penalty for this crime against a theocratic state was death by stoning.

His family wanted to save him; his enemies wanted to destroy him. Both stood on the same ground; namely, that he was mad, that he was other than himself. So Jesus had to face this crisis at different levels.

At one level, he had to deal with the charge that "It is the chief of the demons who gives him the power to drive them [the devils] out" (Mark 3:23, TEV). At another level he had to respond to his family's concern for his mental and spiritual condition.

Jesus' internal struggle is evidenced somewhat in his reply. "How can Satan drive out Satan? If a country divides itself into groups that fight each other, that country will fall apart. If a family divides itself into groups that fight each other, that family will fall apart" (Mark 3:24-25).

To the charge that Satan gave him the power, Jesus responded with the picture of Satan as a strong man bound up in his own house. Then his miracles of healing were cited as evidence that Jesus was the one plundering the Satanic domicile. No, his power did not come from Satan. Rather, Jesus' power came from the source which had broken into Satan's stronghold. This power now acts to liberate all those formerly tyrannized by the devil.

After he demolished the lawyer's arguments, Jesus had to deal with the apprehensions of his own family. This was an authentic crisis, and he had to face the terrible options before him. Should he yield to his family's persuasions, submit to their concerns, give in and go home?

This was not only a crisis in his public ministry, but also a crisis in his personal life as well.

It is not unusual for men to find themselves involved in a personal crisis at the same time that they are called to handle a public crisis.

When Franklin Delano Roosevelt was stricken with polio, his devoted mother insisted that he retire to Hyde Park to lead the sheltered life of a country squire. It took the combined energies of his wife, Eleanor, and his friend Louis Howe, plus his own resolve to remain active in political life, to overcome his mother's well-intentioned insistence.

The situation Jesus faced may be described as "the allegory of the sea voyager." The first man ever to venture out on the sea probably tried to stay in sight of familiar landmarks. As men grew wise in the ways of seafaring, they found new navigational guides in the stars.

The North Star was the sailor's benchmark, the fixed element essential for survival. Then came the day when the sailor, in voyages to the south, completely lost contact with the North Star. Once he entered the Southern Hemisphere, the seafarer was in a totally alien space; his old celestial guide was gone; he was forced to find new cosmic reference points or perish. Some sea voyagers may make mistakes and choose the wrong reference points, for not every star that looks like the North Star is reliable.

What must we do when we move into new hemispheres of our personal and corporate histories? This is what Jesus confronted: The North Star for the Jew had been the Law of Moses, and the Pharisees particularly had devised a complex navigational system to help the Jew in his passage over the high seas of life.

Jesus saw that man was approaching the ethical equator: laws alone would not suffice as mankind entered the new hemisphere; e.g., Jesus actually questioned the Law of Moses: "because of the hardness of your hearts Moses gave you that law" (cf. Mark 10:5). Jesus was searching for new principles, new guiding stars. What are the new hemispheres of our day? Are the long-counted-on North Stars giving way to new ethical codes? To a new morality?

Men whose visions encompass new horizons and hemispheres, whose thoughts commute through new heavens and new laws — such men are often accused of being mad. The apostle Paul won that distinction. Festus cried, "Paul, you are mad." Francis of Assisi was called "mad." The accusation was made against Galileo, Luther, and Jesus. Gandhi must have been mad to take on the mighty British Empire.

Jesus is wrestling here with his own understanding of his mission in life as contrasted with the way his family saw his life work.

To be himself, an individual must do his own deciding. It is in our decision making that we actually become human.

Such is the principle of self-actualizing that the self cannot be divided against itself without injury. In order to have life, the self must remain true to its fundamental moving force if the person is to become actually human.

A word which seems to connect the generations adds a humorous footnote. For some youthful moderns a way-out mode of dress earns the word "crazy," meaning approval. The same garb will get the same word from someone past thirty, but "crazy" now means disapproval.

In the very way in which God created us there is the natural necessity to express an authentic self. This quite proper need may be exaggerated sometimes in modern society. Today, unusual attire and long hair help many a teenager to establish self-identity. Psychologists have linked bizarre dress to the survival of the individual self. Dr. Mary Ellen Roach, of the University of Wisconsin, has written that

> . . . teen-agers in their "search for self" are adventuring into and trying out new modes of behavior within a society which offers many alternatives. Not surprising, therefore, is their susceptibility to fads as they cast about among the alternatives . . . clothes, cosmetics and grooming aids allow each to experiment with the image he wishes to present.[1]

In Jesus' case, his family saw religion as part of the given pattern of life. When Jesus opposed the established religious order, his family began to worry about his emotional stability.

For many people today, as in Jesus' day, a new idea is madness. The scornful charge of madness was brought against Jesus' new ethic of love, which was meant to replace the given ethic of law. We are endlessly told that nobody but a fool would think of anything else in a difficult situation but to "get tough." When we have unrest, use force; when we have discontent, swing a club; when we have demonstrations, put the demonstrators in jail.

It was Albert Schweitzer who alerted us to the realization that Jesus meets us as "an unknown and nameless one," meaning that he comes as one who will not fit into our neat schemes and tidy systems. So, away with him!

When Jesus' idea of God's kingdom threatened to overthrow the tyrant system and the cruel code, he was put away.

He spoke of love and openness while the crowds yelled for law and order; so loved ones thought he must be mad.

Today's troubled society can derive much useful learning from Jesus' personal crisis. He saw that "If a country divides itself into groups that fight each other, that country will fall apart." Just as Abraham Lincoln saw this truth as applicable to the United States in his public debates with Douglas in 1856, so we, too, must recognize its validity.

Whether we find pain or pleasure in gibes of public figures

[1] Mary Ellen Roach, "Adolescent Dress: Understanding the Issues," *Journal of Home Economics,* November, 1969, pp. 693-694.

against youthful dissenters and academic types, as Christians we need to caution the leaders of our national life. Deliberate attempts to turn our nation into two opposing camps may reap short-range political benefits for a few, but in the long run this course leads to national disaster. The same message must go out to militants of the extreme right and left. To the silent majority and to the violent minority, the Christian voice must speak plainly. Our nation, if divided, cannot survive.

Jesus himself did say, "If a family divides itself into groups that fight each other, that family will fall apart" (Mark 3:25, TEV). Wasn't Jesus endangering his own family by refusing their expression of concern?

Jesus had a most difficult choice to make. What did God really want of him? Was his own understanding true to God's calling? Or were his mother and brothers correct in seeing his break with orthodox authority to be a mental vagrancy?

Perhaps there is an autobiographical note in Jesus' words, "A prophet will always be held in honour except in his home town, and among his kinsmen and family" (Mark 6:4, NEB).

Jesus resolutely followed God's call as he knew it. His words must have seemed needlessly harsh to his beloved mother and brothers, but he felt compelled to say that his true relatives are those who obey God.

Can you feel the anguish that Jesus went through before making this pronouncement? It must have cost both Jesus and Mary dearly when he made this hard decision. It is plain, according to Mark, that his mother and brothers failed at this stage to understand Jesus.

Now we come to the third question: What resulted from this critical decision of Jesus?

Until now, we have been thinking about two important truths demonstrated by this crisis in Jesus' life. First, we recognized the home and family to be the basic and original humanizing agency. Our humanity is shaped by our home environment.

Second, the individual, in order to be himself, must do his own deciding, for it is the decision making that makes one's personal growth possible. These are the opposites of our story. In this instance there is a resolution: This crisis which Jesus faced not only spells out the origin of our humanization — the home — and the process of our individualization — decision making — but also the purpose toward which both origin and process direct us.

40

Jesus said, "Who is my mother? Who are my brothers? . . . Here are my mother and brothers. Whoever does the will of God is my brother, my sister, my mother" (cf. Mark 3:33, 35). It is not enough to reject one's family or to remove one's self from the locus of childhood. Such purposeless alienation hinders rather than helps human actualization. Estrangement in itself is both frustrating and futile.

Despite the appearance of the contrary, Jesus did not disown his family. He included his family in a larger brotherhood. What Jesus discovered through this pain-filled experience was that God willed the emergence of a totally new humanity. In Jesus' experience God's reign was not an abstract concept or a theological nicety, but an actual fellowship with men and women who were committed to doing the will of God.

Jesus was able to refuse his family's well-intended counsel because he saw that he, with them, belonged to a more inclusive family. There was to be a new, enlarged family. This family would include anyone who would do the will of the heavenly Father.

In time, Mary and the brothers came to understand this larger meaning of what must have seemed a stern and hard rejection. Mary stood at the foot of the cross. If a family really cares, it is ready to join in the suffering. In the Acts of the Apostles we find Mary and the brothers assembled with the other disciples in Jerusalem.

Jesus' brother James became an influential leader in the first Christian community in Jerusalem. References to his responsible work are found in Acts, Corinthians, and Galatians.

You and I are invited by Jesus Christ to be active in this greater family. Are we ready to feel responsible for those outside our most intimate circle? Are you and I prepared to move beyond the hometown and see the alien, the outsider, as a brother or sister? Are we open to the possibility that God intends that the one I *see* as my enemy really be my brother?

Barbara Ward has shown how mankind has gone through a transition somewhat similar to that of the family. Men first clustered in small groupings which later developed into clans. For a long time these clans were suspicious of each other. Such hostility frequently led to war. Later the loyalty once reserved for the clan was given to nations. Now she says we are becoming aware that we depend on a single environment. We now recognize that earth is just one spaceship. This is forcing

41

us to think beyond national loyalties. At last we are giving serious consideration to the human race as a fraternal community.[2]

In their experience the family of Jesus moved from the *intimate* circle of close family living through the *broken circle,* which came through Joseph's death and Jesus' decision, toward the *larger circle* of a greater family of those who are doing God's will.

Many of us have known similar experiences. Our childhood homes and our early family years, the years of our children's dependence, may have been the intimate circle. Then came the day our children went to school or learned to drive a car or went away to college. The circle was broken.

There now lies before us the larger circle, joining the family of those who want to do God's will.

From intimate circle to broken circle to the larger circle is a pilgrimage. Christ invites us to join the greater family of God's children.

[2] Barbara Ward, *Spaceship Earth* (New York: Columbia University Press, 1966), pp. 140 ff.

42

5. WHEN HIS KING TRIED TO RUB HIM OUT
Luke 9:7-9; 13:31-33; Mark 8:27-33

Other than one's personal family, the political state is the largest single influence on the individual's life and destiny. The government registers our birth, oversees our education, conscripts our sons to fight her wars, and collects taxes from our estates even after we are dead. Not even the church is as prodigal in her claims upon the believer as is the state in its demands upon her citizens.

What should our relationship, as Christians, be to the ever-increasing power of the governing state? Perhaps this crisis in the personal history of Jesus may throw some light upon our personal responsibility toward the ruling powers.

Let us examine this crisis by sorting out Herod's confusion, Jesus' conviction, and Peter's confession.

Let's look first at Herod's confusion. In Luke's Gospel we find Herod saying, "I had John's head cut off; but who is this man I hear these things about?" (Luke 9:9, TEV). A brief description of this Herod is in order. Herod Antipas was the son of Herod the Great, the king in Jerusalem who figured in the Christmas stories and was responsible for the massacre of the babies reported in Matthew 2. After the death of Herod, Antipas was made king over the territory of Galilee and Peraea. He ruled until A.D. 29. His immorality matched that of his infamous father. John the Baptist had rebuked the prince for violating the Jewish Law in divorcing his wife and marrying his brother's wife. This prophetic denunciation brought a jail sentence. Later the despot ordered John's execution.

After that, when Herod heard all that was going on, he was bewildered. Herod exclaimed, "John, I beheaded; but who is this . . . ?" (Luke 9:9, RSV).

Tyranny is always perplexed by the persistence and stubbornness of faithful men and religious movements. Religious faith generates a power of resistance with which the weapons of despotism cannot cope. Herod thought he had settled the prophetic movement within his land by executing John the Baptizer. Such is the error of all dictators who think that the sword can suppress truth.

This may be called the Herod syndrome: "I had John's head

43

cut off; but who is this man?" The abusers of power never can understand why the badly misused and the greatly abused continue to demand what is rightly theirs.

In 1970, more than one hundred years after the American Civil War, the Gallup Poll indicated that white Americans feel that the progress of integration is too fast. Is it too fast for those black students who sat helplessly in a school bus while a white mob overturned it? Is it too fast for a welfare mother in Kansas City who has eighteen cents per meal per child per day? Is it too fast for those black children in Mississippi who have grown well past their puberty since the Supreme Court first decided that the United States Constitution guaranteed them a right to equal education? Still, a child's lifetime later, the school system is not providing that birthright! Is this too fast?

The political system of democracy was developed to protect the citizen from the very real danger of tyranny. The essence of democracy is accountability. All elected officials must be held accountable. Even the president of the United States is not outside this necessary principle. His declarations, especially, must conform to the facts.

On one day in the early seventies, this nation's chief executive officer officially declared that we had no ground forces in the neutral country of Laos. Had twenty-four hours passed before the Department of Defense admitted that our nation had been paying combat pay to our forces in Laos since 1966? As an active army officer then said to me: "At least we can now acknowledge the men who died in honorable service of their country. Until now, for political reasons, we could not recognize their deaths." If the editors of the leading newspapers of our land refuse to pay heed to this wide gap of distortion between the solemn declarations of the commander in chief and the belated admissions of the Defense Department, then perhaps, as in the days of ancient Israel, the backwoods preachers should begin immediately to demand truthfulness from the heads of state.

A credibility gap exists whenever we have less than honest, less than complete, statements from officials in high public office. Credibility gap is also the euphemism used when a high public official is caught telling a lie.

What is my Christian responsibility in this matter? Perhaps I have been conditioned by my childhood. I remember the rise of Nazi Germany. Fine Christians in Germany fell into step

44

as Germany occupied the Saar. Hardly a congregation stirred as Hitler took over Austria. Not many prophetic voices spoke out as Hitler invaded Poland. Where was the voice of Christian conscience when the Nazis built assembly lines to lessen the production costs for mass murder?

Let me be very clear. I am not saying that our president or any former president is a Herod or a Hitler or even a tyrant. I am saying only what Lord Acton said: "Power corrupts — absolute power corrupts absolutely."

I happen to think that Lyndon Baines Johnson and Richard Milhous Nixon are dedicated and sincere men. Either is as trustworthy as any living person.

The difference between Lyndon Johnson and Richard Nixon and yourself and myself is this: The U.S. president has at his fingertips the greatest accumulation of power available to any single man in the world today. I would not trust myself, nor would I trust any living person, with such power. The *Christian Science Monitor* has stated editorially: "Today's President is much more than the presiding officer contemplated and intended by the Founding Fathers. He comes very close to being an elected emperor." [1] The founding fathers of our nation had great wisdom in putting the control of our federal government

NOT in the hands of the president alone,

NOT in the hands of the Congress alone,

NOT in the hands of the courts alone.

They separated the powers because they knew that wherever power concentrates, there tyranny lurks. This is why deceit is so dangerous to a democracy. Truth is essential if power is not to degenerate into tyranny.

Our society moves dangerously close to another trap whenever instances such as the following occur. Under the guise of preventing danger to visiting dignitaries and to our own president, a recent Administration asked Congress to bar public demonstrations. Some observers at the time pointed out that such a law would effectively shield the presidential eyes from any dissent that might annoy or discomfit him.

Now, the president deserves to have his own person protected from physical dangers. As a Christian, I have denounced and now again denounce the hate-filled violence that has assassinated some of our finest national leaders.

[1] "On the Presidency," *The Christian Science Monitor* (Boston), May 25, 1971.

Protect the presidential person, yes! Protect the protesters as well!

Why should we as Christians be so concerned about recent political happenings? Christians historically have had a peculiar intuition about history. We believe in the continuing work of God in history. You might call it our politicalized doctrine of the Holy Spirit.

If God is to work his will in human affairs, then the processes of social organization and government must be open to the input of truth from whatever source. So free churchmen since John Bunyan have seen persuasion as an essential tool in influencing society. To persuade, our eyes, ears, minds, and voices must be active.

We must be alert to what is happening. We must be abreast of political events. We must be ready to risk confrontation, for a healthy society leaves room for an honest examination of the facts. A democratic society must be an open society. A living democracy must allow plenty of elbowroom for the expressions of conscience. Silencing the pulpit, closing down the lecture hall, and sealing off peaceful public assembly leads to tyranny. To close off debate by deceit or brute force is to shut down the operation of democracy, whether it is initiated by the tough tactics of the radical students or the thin skins of those in political power.

Herod's confusion was to think that the strong man decides history. Modern men and societies continue to share in Herod's confusion. Not only among the foolishness of the comic pages do we find the slogan "Law and Order First," but also we hear these chilling words on the political banquet circuit. "Law and Order First," if understood according to the exact value that the words suggest, describes a dictatorship, not a democracy. The nation that earnestly desires domestic tranquillity needs more justice in the land, not just more armed men in the streets.

In a certain Arab country the ruling prince attempted to discourage stealing by cutting off the right hands of the offenders. The net result was a great number of one-handed thieves. He might have had better results if he had shared part of his princely wealth with the poor and created a more just society where stealing was not essential to survival.

Herod thought, because he held the power of life and death over his subjects, that he possessed the means to force their allegiance. Jesus refused to be frightened. With the scornful

46

words "Tell that fox" (Luke 13:32), he dismissed the terrible, destructive powers of the ruthless tyrant. It is difficult, if not impossible, to intimidate the man or woman fully committed to God's purpose. The person of faith is unafraid of "those who kill the body but cannot afterward do anything worse" (Luke 12:4, TEV). The religious man's only concern is to be loyal to truth, justice, and love. Herod could not intimidate Jesus. Jesus' only concern was that he not betray the trust he had from God.

In this chapter we are looking at only a small part of the crisis Jesus confronted in his own life. The larger issue was the question of direction for Jesus' mission. What exactly did God want Jesus to do? When Jesus knew this direction better, he had to consider how he was to communicate this difficult mission to his disciples. They still had wrong notions concerning the Messiah. We will not examine these questions but rather the circumstances surrounding the acute crisis.

The evidence of Jesus' conviction is found in such words as, "I must journey on today, tomorrow and the next day. . . ." (See Luke 13:31-33, Phillips.) Jesus did not interrupt his ministry because of any fear of Herod. Earlier Jesus had said, "The Son of Man has no place to lie down and rest." Now comes the solemn declaration, "It is not right for a prophet to be killed anywhere except in Jerusalem" (Luke 13:33, TEV). Though he may have scornfully dismissed Herod's threat, Jesus realized that his days in Galilee were numbered.

We might think that Jesus stoically recognized his fate and accepted it. Not so, reading Mark's Gospel carefully, we find that Jesus left Galilee and moved to the north, the opposite direction from Jerusalem. Was Jesus another prophet like Jonah, refusing God's commission to preach the saving word to Nineveh? Not at all; the Scriptures do not suggest this. Rather Jesus used this time to sort out the various alternatives; it was a respite that allowed him to examine the options, an interlude during which he reexamined his life mission.

These must have been trying days for Jesus. Often when we are really in a mess, we are forced to make some of the most important decisions of our lives. All at once Jesus found himself under pressure from the Pharisees, his life threatened by Herod, and his disciples distracted by fears and anxieties as well as fanciful illusions of impending greatness.

Jesus apparently made his critical decision alone, but he

was not entirely alone. God was present, and the fellowship of the disciples was at least supportive. The disciples may not have understood him, but they went along with him. God's presence was real since Jesus seems to have been of the conviction that God is in control of history.

With the words "It is not right for a prophet . . ." Jesus plainly indicated that he saw himself as standing in the prophetic tradition of the Hebrew prophets.

The Hebrew prophets were men who could see God's guiding hand in the human affairs of their times. Amos saw God's purpose at work in the international and national scene. He declared that Yahweh demanded justice and mercy in human affairs. Hosea warned Israel against the disaster of forming alliances with Egypt and Assyria. Isaiah saw God as more powerful than the mightiest of conquering nations. Jeremiah denounced the popular notion that God never would allow his chosen people to be destroyed by the enemy. The events of history demonstrated that these prophets had read correctly the signs of God's activity in human events.

Some persons would suggest that Jesus had no views on the political issues of his day. However, his description of Herod as "that fox" certainly indicates that he had political opinions. Indeed, he was rather effective in expressing such public views. Besides being a word which serves as a metaphor for a cunning man, "fox" in rabbinical literature means an unimportant individual. It is a term of contempt.

> It takes a brave man to call the reigning king a fox. It is told that [Hugh] Latimer was once preaching in Westminster Abbey when Henry the king was one of his congregation. In the pulpit [Latimer] soliloquised, "Latimer! Latimer! Latimer! Be careful what you say. The king of England is here!" Then he went on, "Latimer! Latimer! Latimer! Be careful what you say. The King of Kings is here." [2]

We are told that Psalm 118 was one of Jesus' favorites. A verse from that Psalm reads: "With the Lord on my side I do not fear. What can man do to me?" (Psalm 118:6). Since the time of Jesus, many of his followers have come to share his conviction that God is hard at work in the affairs of men. Faithful men hold some values more dear than life itself. Tyrants have never been able to understand this. The heroic deaths of faith-filled men have provided a legacy of witnesses

[2] William Barclay, ed., *The Gospel of Luke* (Philadelphia: The Westminster Press, 1957), pp. 191-192.

48

to the truth that God does somehow intrude himself into human events.

During the reign of Queen Mary in England (1553-1558), many English reformers became martyrs. Two of them were Hugh Latimer and Nicholas Ridley, who were burned as heretics on October 16, 1555. History records that

> . . . when Bishops Ridley and Latimer were being bound to the stake, Latimer said to his friend: "Be of good cheer, Master Ridley, and play the man, for we shall this day light such a candle in England as I trust by God's grace shall never be put out." [3]

Where did Jesus' journey take him? According to the itinerary in Mark's Gospel, Jesus first went north toward Tyre and Sidon. These two cities are on the Mediterranean Coast, about the top of the map in our Bible maps of the Holy Land. Then Jesus moved east, inland, and began slowly to turn south. He did not go back by way of his native Galilee. As he undertook his journey to Jerusalem, he first moved near the city of Caesarea-Philippi. As the name suggests, this is a city which was dedicated in honor of the Roman emperor and was located in the domain of King Philip, another of the sons of the terrible Herod the Great.

In primitive times, the pagan god Pan had been worshiped here. Pan had been the Greek god of the forests, the flocks, and the herds. Some suggest that the notion of the devil popular in the Dark Ages was based on Pan. In the time of Jesus, the emperor was worshiped by loyal Romans.

It was in this haunt of pagan worship, amid the shrines of both Pan and Caesar, that Jesus asked the question of his disciples, "Who do you say that I am?" Amid the ancient idols Peter answered him, "You are the Christ" (Mark 8:29). You are the one whom God has anointed to set the people free. Thus Peter pronounced the death sentence upon all the gods which stood before him, not one of whom could save mankind.

Peter confessed, "You are the Messiah" (NEB). In recognizing Jesus as the one sent by God, Peter was confessing, "I'll risk my life on your conviction." Peter ventured forth after Jesus. He shared the same conviction that God is active as a liberating force in the affairs of men and nations. Today we find many personalities, many societies who have yet to discover that the old gods are long dead.

[3] Winthrop S. Hudson, *The Story of the Christian Church* (New York: Harper & Row, Publishers, 1958), p. 59.

Our word "panic" comes from the Greek god Pan. This is a sudden overwhelming fear, often without cause, that produces irrational behavior. Such panic often spreads quickly through a group of persons or animals.

Many people today are responding to contemporary events as though they had been frightened by the devil or by Pan himself. We see mature men reacting without logic or reason. We find entire movements within our society that might be called "Members of the Order of the Panic Button." We see certain personalities frantically pushing a button that is supposed to set everything back in order just the way things were before everything seems to have gone wrong.

Devotees of the god Pan can be found on the far right, as well as the far left, of human society. Pan has his fans among the young as well as the old.

Peter's confession, "Jesus, you are the Christ," can mean this to those prone to panic: Pan is long dead. The world is in safe hands. God is at the helm of history. Look about you now for the signs as God works setting persons free.

There are many, many who have not heard the good news that Caesar is dead and that Caesar worship is worthless. It is true that Caesar worship now comes in new, up-to-date models, but it is still the same old dead and deadly stuff. Caesar worship comes in two familiar packages. One is narrow nationalism, and the other is modern militarism. There are variations on the basic models, such as the military-industrial-university complex. You can even have Caesar worship, nationalistic style, in a very mini-economy size. You aren't required to do anything or be anything. You just take this little Caesar religious emblem and paste it on your window. Actually, there is a very popular creedal statement of Caesar worship: "Love Caesar or leave Caesar's land."

To the worshipers of military might comes the word of judgment. Your gods are dead. They are incapable of producing life. They can deliver only more death.

To those who are ready to confess that the gods Pan and Caesar are dead, that the world can live only if the Lord of Life is proclaimed, comes the question, "Who do you say that I am?"

Jesus accepted from his disciples the title "The Lord's anointed." At the same time he tried to teach them that his work was not one of conquest. Rather, he and his followers

50

were called to serve. Our calling is to respond in supreme obedience to the will of God. We are part of a mission of service and sacrifice, not of ease and glory.

Herod was only confused by what he heard that Jesus was saying and doing. Peter, on the opposite hand, was ready to confess, "You are the Lord's anointed."

Are we ready to share with Jesus in his conviction that God is in control of history? Are we ready to affirm, "I'll risk my life on Jesus' conviction?" Are we ready to live as free men in a world where God continues to set persons and institutions free from old tyrannies?

If our response is yes, then let us go about living as liberated men and women working to make our society more free, giving of ourselves that a greater number of our fellow citizens might recognize the true dimensions of freedom, risking ourselves in confrontation that Americans, and all mankind, might truly live as free men in free societies.

The choice is before us: We can remain part of Herod's confusion and refuse to acknowledge God's saving hand at work in our affairs, or we can join Peter in confessing Christ. Let's go out together to tell everybody that this is really a free society, because God is making it so.

6. WHEN THEY DISAPPROVED OF THE COMPANY HE KEPT
Luke 7:31-35

If "crisis" describes a state of affairs out of which a decisive change for better or worse is bound to happen, then the situation resulting from the kind of pals Jesus picked surely fits the word. The company Jesus kept caused a definite turning point in the course of his religious ministry. By his decision to serve as a physician among the really sick people, Jesus broke with the prevailing religious attitudes of his day.

We live in a day when many different styles of life compete for our loyalties. Jesus himself lived in a world similar to ours in its fast-moving changes. A study of the companions he chose and the reasons for his choices may assist us as we agonize over the options we face regarding different kinds of people and life-styles.

In this chapter we will examine three questions regarding Jesus' choice of companions:

What kind of company did Jesus keep?

Why did he keep such company?

What is appropriate company for one of God's people?

First, what kind of company did Jesus keep? The Gospel accounts provide a fairly accurate record of Jesus' acquaintances. Jesus, himself, repeated the accusations lodged against him. "Look at this man! He is a glutton and wine-drinker, and is a friend of tax collectors and outcasts!" (Luke 7:34, TEV).

This verse probably describes with accuracy how the Pharisees and canonical lawyers felt about Jesus. At the same time Jesus showed little concern about correcting their impression. Such a description obviously shows some distortion, especially since it is drawn in such sharp contrast with the austere life-style of John the Baptist.

Jesus seemed not to care about how they represented him because, quite likely, he had already weighed the consequences of undertaking his particular kind of ministry. By choosing to go to the socially disinherited, he recognized that he would be inviting misunderstanding. The strictly religious persons avoided contact with the irreligious in order not to be contaminated by such idolatrous sinners. They noticed that Jesus was so careless in his associations that he endangered his own religious clean-

52

ness. No Pharisee was likely to label Jesus as "clean Gene." Jesus had too many of the wrong kinds of friends for that. When some religious instructors observed Jesus at a meal, they were offended that he would eat in such bad company.

The religious elite in Palestine regarded many of Jesus' companions as beyond the borders of God's concern. In John 7:49, we read that some Pharisees were saying, "But this crowd, who do not know the law, are accursed." It was precisely to such outsiders that Jesus chose to minister. Jesus described his mission in this way: "I have not come to call the respectable people, but the outcasts" (Mark 2:17, TEV).

Who were some of these dispossessed? To begin with the best of the list, the Gospels note that Jesus befriended women. Now the modern mind easily grasps the ceremonial reason why strictly religious individuals would be offended by anyone regularly seen in bad company. But what's wrong with women friends? One need not go as far back as the first century to find women cut off from normal society. The present day furnishes ample evidence that women are still treated as a subspecies. The right to vote and to hold property was "granted" to women only quite recently, and still does not exist in many nations. We are just beginning to recognize the variety of built-in prejudices against women in our western nations. For example, we have yet to deal with the reasons why so many professions are closed to women. Why are there the double standards in salaries and in status?

Indeed, the first-century Jewish woman was better protected by Judaism's laws than was the average Hellenistic woman of the Roman world. Certainly many Jewish injunctions were intended for the woman's well-being. However, one of the most deeply ingrained and prejudicial assumptions of males is their supposedly innate superiority to the female *homo sapiens*. This is so today, and it was more so in Jesus' day. The fact that he had so many women friends did not help his claim to be a religious teacher, certainly not with his professional associates.

"You wouldn't expect that John the Baptist would allow women to travel across the countryside with him, would you? You don't see Gamaliel or Hillel allowing women to enroll in their classes, do you? Certainly not! Women have their place, and they ought to stay in it." Jesus was offending all sorts of social taboos by allowing women to follow him in his travels and contribute to his expenses.

53

Here is how Luke describes it: "After this he went journeying from town to town and village to village, proclaiming the good news of the kingdom of God. With him were the Twelve and a number of women who had been set free from evil spirits and infirmities: Mary, known as Mary of Magdala, from whom seven devils had come out, Joanna, the wife of Chuza a steward of Herod's, Susanna, and many others. These women provided for them out of their own resources" (Luke 8:1-3, NEB).

It is truly remarkable that a first-century man could have such an open attitude toward women. Such acceptance of females stands in startling contrast to the cruel and callous attitude of the Roman world toward all human life. The Hellenistic empire accorded little worth to a woman. The cultural mores actively promoted homosexual relations between males. To the Hellenized Roman, the primary function of a woman was to bear children.

Jesus' many associations with women are rooted in the healthier attitude of first-century Jewish males. Jesus gave dignity to the relations between men and women. Women were worth engaging in conversation as when Jesus visited with Martha and Mary (Luke 10:38-42). Women had something to say, and Jesus listened to the woman at the well (John 4:7-42). Evidence that Jesus paid close attention to what was said to him occurs in the interchange which Luke records: ". . . a woman spoke up from the crowd and said to him, 'How happy is the woman who bore you and nursed you!'" (Luke 11:27, TEV). Jesus responded by correcting her intended blessing into the striking rejoinder, "No, happy are those who hear the word of God and keep it" (Luke 11:28, NEB).

Perhaps the spiritual elite of Palestine only raised their eyebrows at Jesus' women companions, but they had more harsh words about the bad characters who hung around him. Of course some of these "no goods" happened to be women. Luke reports about such an occasion. "A Pharisee invited Jesus to have dinner with him. . . . There was a woman in that town who lived a sinful life" (Luke 7:36-37, TEV). Probably she had been a prostitute. Jesus' ministry apparently had touched her life, for when she heard that Jesus was eating in the Pharisee's house, she immediately went there. She carried an alabaster jar full of perfume. The Pharisee apparently missed the significance of her conduct. Like so many of us, his thinking was one dimensional. A devoutly religious man, he lived the

54

style of life required of him by his religious teachers. He deliberately avoided contact with such sinful characters as this woman of the street. In this case he responded naturally by feeling himself superior to Jesus. His conscious thought was to feel mildly sorry for his guest. "If this man really were a prophet, he would know who this woman is who is touching him; he would know what kind of sinful life she leads!" (Luke 7:39, TEV). How surprised he must have been when Jesus took him to task as an inhospitable host who failed to provide the customary services afforded visitors! More shocking must have been Jesus' accusation that he was a pious stuffed shirt who failed to recognize the forgiving love of God even when it took place in his own home and before his very own eyes.

Many congregations identify themselves by names, such as, "Church of the Master" or "Church of Our Savior." If we were to confess our true condition, we might designate ourselves "Church of the Pious Pharisee" or "Church of the Insensitive Scribe." As a modern-day Christian, I, for one, have often missed observing God's saving activity because my eyes were blinded by the presence of the sinner. As though there was ever to be forgiveness without someone seeking to be forgiven!

This woman was not alone on the list of bad characters with whom Jesus' name was linked. If there was a Pharisee's Bureau of Investigation, their files on Jesus would have included such information as this: "Undercover Agent Z reports that Jesus was seen in the company of tax collectors and outcasts." "Agent 7 5/8 reports that Jesus invited himself to go home with Zacchaeus, who has grown rich by taxing the citizens. Zacchaeus is known as a collaborator with the Roman authorities and has systematically cheated Jewish citizens" (see Luke 19:1-10). Among the notations in the PBI files might have been one: "Fifteen drachmas paid to informer who said, 'This man welcomes outcasts and even eats with them!'" (see Luke 15:2, TEV).

The case against Jesus is undeniable. He himself acknowledged that he had heard the rumor with which his opposition had tried to slander him. They were calling him "a glutton and wine-drinker." Jesus had heard the accusations, and still he continued to associate with despised tax collectors and to make friends among the outcasts. Why was Jesus so interested in known publicans and hard-core sinners? Why did he keep such company?

In fairness to the Pharisees, it must be noted that they were trying to do what sincere religious persons always have tried to do — be good churchmen. Their religious code was very clear — don't mix, don't mess with the morally dispossessed. The Pharisees recognized the good intentions of Jesus; he was obviously as sincere in his religious faith as they were in theirs. But why did Jesus behave so differently? Finally some of the bewildered Pharisees and teachers of the Law came to him with their complaint. "'Why do you eat and drink with tax collectors and outcasts?' they asked" (Luke 5:30, TEV). The first part of any answer to their question must have been fairly apparent. Had they been able to get past their own hang-ups, the religious critics might have noticed that it was mainly the less respectable types who were ready to accept Jesus' help. These were people with pressing needs. They had been cut off from society. The religious establishment saw them as outcasts. Jesus opened himself to them for he saw them as sinners in need of care.

The religion which both the Pharisees and Jesus had been taught, for theirs was a single heritage, stressed the availability of God's forgiving love to the repentant sinner. The established religious leadership waited for the sinner to come confessing his waywardness. The religious code provided appropriate ways for restoring the repentant to his rightful place in the community of the faithful.

What was new in Jesus' ministry was that he sought out the sinner. He went looking for those who had been disowned by the "better classes." Jesus delighted in telling of the shepherd who was good because he searched for the lost sheep. Sorry to say, Jesus' way of doing things may have introduced a new religion, but it is a poor way of doing business. Sound religion, in Jesus' day as well as in ours, is practical business. A hundred sheep represented a big capital investment. It is unlikely that the owner would praise the shepherd who left ninety-nine sheep behind, no matter how good those sheep dogs were supposed to be. Rather lose the one than risk the ninety-nine — that's sound business. Don't talk of the "good" shepherd — that kind of one-against-ninety-nine thinking represents poor business risks.

Yet Jesus remained firm in his insistence that the deprived must be restored. How enthusiastically Jesus told his audience of the woman who dropped all her household responsibilities and did nothing but search for that lost coin. Note that the

56

trilogy of stories of the lost sheep, the lost coin, and the lost son were told in response to the criticism, "This man welcomes outcasts and even eats with them!" (See Luke 15:1-32, TEV.) Jesus really meant it. He saw his ministry as providing care for the disinherited. The Pharisees were both practical and devout, and they recognized the danger as well as expense in such religious aspirations. There was the danger of being contaminated by the very people you were trying to aid. It would be a very real expense to any religious institution that attempted to serve the many needs of the dispossessed.

One of the outstanding characteristics of the Second Vatican Council of the Catholic Church was the strong and repeated emphasis upon concern for the earth's poor. The missionary bishops from South America, Asia, and Africa again and again urged that this great Christian church prepare to "lose its life" in order to reach out and lift up the downtrodden. The fervent speeches of the bishops clearly recognized the high cost of such a ministry. They called for the church to assume the servant style of Jesus Christ.

Jesus spelled out the reason behind his conscious decision to take upon himself this dangerous and expensive servanthood. "People who are well do not need a doctor, but only those who are sick. Go and find out what this scripture means, 'I do not want animal sacrifices, but kindness.' For I have not come to call the respectable people, but the outcasts" (Matthew 9: 12-13, TEV).

That's an unforgettable image — a physician who moves out to heal the really sick people. But Jesus was so unrealistic. Where do today's medical school graduates go? To places where illness is most severe, to urban slums, to impoverished towns and backward rural areas? Most of today's doctors set up their practices among the people who can afford to pay for their services. We cannot be too hard on the young medics because our churches do the same. Where have the churches made their cutbacks in time of economic recession? In large part, they scaled down on their missionary giving. Good, religious folk reduced what they gave to care for the outsider. Yesterday's Pharisee and today's churchman find Jesus' words strange. His sayings make us feel a trifle guilty. Any one of us might become defensive regarding what seems to be an accusation. How sincere am I in my professed dedication to Jesus when I honestly face the comparison between what I spend to clothe, shelter,

57

feed, transport, and entertain myself (and my loved ones) and what I spend to aid and comfort the less fortunate among my brothers in God's human family?

As have many novelists before him, John Fowles has described English Victorian society of the late nineteenth century in his *The French Lieutenant's Woman*. He draws his reader's attention to the subordinate place that society accorded to women, household servants, and the working class. The economically well-off accepted their class superiority as a condition apparently ordained in creation. The emerging consciousness of less fortunate social and economic classes was branded as poor manners or disloyalty to the nation.

Many novelists as well as social historians have recorded how the upper classes used both the national flag and Christian religion in defense of their privileged positions. Small wonder, then, that the bulk of Europe's industrial workers have become estranged from the churches. For too long Christendom has been identified too closely with the ruling social classes. The thought patterns of the Pharisees were not limited to the first century. Wherever and whenever men put privilege before human service, their conduct is more like the religious elite of Jesus' day than it is like the founder's model for a Christian servant community. This raises the issue: What is appropriate company for the churches to keep? The question and any response assume that man is born a responsible creature. Part of such responsibility is expressed in what commitments are made to one's fellows and to the source of all life and goodness, God.

The Pharisees attempted to resolve this by seeing the company of God-fearing men as an exclusive society. By committing oneself to a rigorous ethic, a person demonstrated that he deserved membership among the elect. His conduct was above criticism, and he selected his company from among those who shared in his strict religious code. This pious fraternity was open to as many as were willing to undertake the stern requirements. This model is a most effective way of organizing for religious purposes. It allowed Judaism to survive as a healthy religious organism in a decaying age. Christians owe an immense debt to these, our elder brothers in the faith. From the trunk of first-century Judaism the Christian branch grew.

The closely organized, strictly disciplined model functioned well, especially in times of peril. Ignatius Loyola established the Society of Jesus on very strict and exclusive lives. This highly disciplined order played a major role in the Counter-Reformation which saved vast areas of Europe for the Catholic Church.

The Reformation itself was not without its exclusiveness. The power of John Calvin's Reformed Churches gained speed and movement from their sense of exclusiveness. What else are "the elect" but a special class?

John Wesley organized a disciplined band out of which grew one of the most virile and fruitful communions of the Christian world, the Methodist Church.

In the present day can a precise answer be found easily to the question "What kind of companions ought a Christian to have?" Certainly the way we organize modern churches is to make joining as easy as possible for practically anybody. This is not doing necessarily what Jesus did and what he invited his disciples to do. Having low standards for membership is not quite the same as actively going out to provide care for those outcasts who most need it.

Jesus' own answer to this question is worth noting. "God's wisdom, however, is shown to be true by all who accept it" (Luke 7:35, TEV). The children of wisdom must have included the publicans and sinners whom Jesus was accused of befriending. This saying of Jesus may be interpreted in various ways, but certainly the prostitute who anointed his feet, whom Jesus pronounced to be forgiven, and who began a totally new way of life demonstrated God's wisdom.

Our modern societies sorely need to recover this great concern Jesus showed for the dispossessed. Whether one travels in Chicago or Calcutta, Manhattan or Marseilles, the sensitive person is surely aware that the greatest waste of our natural endowment is the misuse we make of human resources. To watch a child at play among the littered streets and to imagine what the next ten years of that child's life will be like forces the questions, "Who *cares* about this child? Who will attend to his needs? Who will come to his aid?" God's wisdom surely will be proven by those who accept it and carry it out. What of those who identify themselves as modern-day followers of Jesus? What are we doing to put into practice Jesus' concern for the outcasts? Or are we using our energies to make absolutely sure that the outsider does not move into our neighborhood?

To put the matter affirmatively, we may look at some of the positive measures taken to improve the condition of the deprived persons. Poverty in modern societies often reduces educational opportunities. Governments have initiated programs, such as, "Upward Bound," which enrich the learning experiences of young persons. One young educator found the program a wonderful way of expressing his Christian ministry. Spending time with young students, sharing books, opening new opportunities, such as attending an orchestral concert or a choral recital, visiting museums and art galleries, pushed wide the mental horizons of these high schoolers. One year of such personal efforts produced amazing results. Some students who would otherwise have known only the changeless, besieged world of poverty and ignorance discovered immense new areas of interest and growth. The governmental program helped, of course. However, the key to the rapid development of these young people was in the personal interest and concern demonstrated by their special teacher.

Here, quite obviously, is an important place for the sincere Christian to invest himself. There are still many "excluded" persons, young and old, who will not be admitted into society until some insider willingly shares of what he has in order that the other might experience belonging.

A thirteen-year-old girl was on a spring tour with her junior high chorus. This took the singing group into a city in western Canada. Upon her return, she related some of her experiences to her family. She told of the first night when the students went out in threes and fours to restaurants for dinner. Her little gang chose to eat fish and chips, English style. "There was a lot to eat," she reported, "and the food was kind of greasy, but that's not what made some of us sick." "What was it?" her parents anxiously inquired. "When we were coming back to our nice hotel, we passed a man who was rummaging for food in the garbage cans outside the back door of the restaurant. Then we thought of all the food we had left on our plates inside, and here he was outside digging to the bottom of those barrels of garbage; it made us so sick."

This was a most unpleasant experience. How might her parents have responded to her expressions of concern? The content of such a response would have indicated how serious their awareness of Jesus' driving compassion for the socially shortchanged was.

What kinds of friends should a Christian have? Perhaps that answer might best be put in these terms. Appropriate company for a Christian is any person who needs to be helped. The

60

Christian's friends are those whose needs require personal attention. The disciple of Christ cares enough to try to provide new health to those who need it. How would you describe the right kind of company for a Christian to keep?

In 1944, the armed forces of Germany were just beginning to fall back before the pressures of the allied forces. This did not prevent the German leader, Adolf Hitler, from pressing forward in his aim to destroy Europe's Jews. He insisted that the nations yoked in the fascist cause begin to murder their Jewish populations. One such satellite state was Hungary. The world leaders, such as Pope Pius, pleaded with the Hungarian government to halt the deportation of its Jewish subjects. To be deported meant certain death. U.S. President Franklin D. Roosevelt threatened to bomb Hungary if the deportations were not stopped.

More influential than either pope or president was one imaginative young man, a Swede named Raoul Wallenberg. His story is recorded by Arthur Morse in his book entitled *While Six Million Died*.[1] Sweden was a neutral nation whose goodwill was eagerly sought by all nations. This allowed Swedish businessmen some freedom to travel into wartime countries. On such business trips, the thirty-two-year-old Wallenberg became aware of the brutality of the Nazis and the tragic condition of the Jews.

Sweden had been aroused over the desperate situation of Europe's Jews, and governmental offices cooperated with private organizations in setting up a rescue operation. Lively and clever Raoul was an important key in this humanitarian effort.

When he arrived in Budapest, he found that the Swedish diplomatic minister had already issued six hundred provisional passports to Jews who had some personal or business ties with Sweden. Wallenburg printed a fancy passport which featured official seals and Sweden's triple-crown insignia. This document extended the protection of the Swedish government to any who carried it. Then the young man talked Hungarian officials into accepting as valid five thousand of these passes.

But life for the Jews of Budapest was still very dangerous. They were still subject to attacks in the streets from city policemen and armed gangs of Fascist Arrow Cross members.

So Wallenberg began to build a city of life for the Jews

[1] Arthur D. Morse, *While Six Million Died* (New York: Random House, Inc., 1968), p. 371.

61

within the city that spelled death for them. Working without resting, he organized a city-wide relief operation complete with nurseries, soup kitchens, and hospitals. Four hundred Jews were hired to run these life-giving institutions. Food, clothing, and medicine were purchased. Wallenberg risked his own life, but so anxious were the Germans and Hungarians to keep open their contacts with neutral Sweden that they took no action against the active rescuer of human life. Indeed, Hungarian officials allowed him to distribute an additional five thousand of his protective passports.

Eventually, the Swedish rescue program sheltered twenty thousand Jews. Wallenberg recruited forty doctors who inoculated the closely crowded ghetto residents against the serious dangers of cholera, typhoid, and paratyphoid.

His resourcefulness is demonstrated in this one scene, which was played over and over again. The German troops tried to put together trainloads of Jews to ship back to Germany. Wallenberg had set up his own alert system which would notify him of their efforts to round up Jews for deportation. Again and again he would show up at the station and bluff the guards into releasing Jews. On one occasion he used his Swedish credentials to rescue three hundred Jews. He simply marched them away from the railroad station.

He himself was spirited away to Russia when the Russians occupied Hungary in the closing days of the war. The conquerors were suspicious of anybody who could exert this much influence. He was never seen alive again. One person wrote of him: "Whatever his actual fate, Wallenberg left a rich legacy — the lives of more than a hundred thousand Jews." [2]

How about it? What is appropriate company for a Christian? In what ways did Jesus respond to such a question? As you think through the unusual friends Jesus attracted and especially as you reflect upon just why he spent his time and energies with the socially unacceptable, you may find new understandings regarding the style of friendship that may rightly be called Christian.

[2] *Ibid.*

62

7. WHEN JESUS BROKE WITH TRADITION
Mark 7:1-13

Tradition is essential for the growth and development of both the person and the society. At the same time, tradition often blocks the full development possible for that person or that society. Sometimes the question is asked: "Why do we do what we do?" The answer too often is "tradition."

Under what circumstances, if any, does a person break with tradition? Jesus faced this crisis in his life. How did he respond to that which had been handed down to him? Perhaps we can gain insights into our own decision making by examining how Jesus dealt with tradition. We will consider three questions:

How did Jesus affirm tradition?

How did Jesus break with the inherited past?

What price do we have to pay when we either affirm tradition or break it?

Recognizing the essential value of tradition, this handing down of beliefs and customs from generation to generation is terribly important. It virtually identifies man as a rational and social creature.

Every culture depends upon this transmission of past into present, whether the repetition is by word of mouth or by practice. Continuity with the past gives present experience its texture and quality.

What do we do about what we are given by those who guide and instruct us?

Looking at Jesus and his response to this very human situation, we note that Jesus inherited a rich religious tradition. Among the Jews, tradition described an unwritten body of laws which God had given to Moses at Sinai. This code had been handed down from generation to generation, first by word of mouth and then in written form. Jesus recognized the importance of his inheritance. In Luke's Gospel is evidence of his great dependence upon the long established institutions of Judaism. Luke recorded that ". . . on the Sabbath day he went as usual to the synagogue. He stood up to read the Scriptures . . ." (Luke 4:16, TEV).

Here is plain proof that Jesus affirmed at least three of the four basic institutions of Judaism — the sabbath, the synagogue, and the Scriptures. But what about the fourth basic foundation of Judaism — the Torah, that is, the Law?

We know how Jesus felt about the basic religious law of his people because he tells us in his own words. "Do not think that I have come to do away with the Law of Moses and the teachings of the prophets. I have not come to do away with them, but to give them real meaning. Remember this!" (Matthew 5:17, 18a, TEV). "So long as heaven and earth endure, not a letter, not a stroke, will disappear from the Law until all that must happen has happened" (Matthew 5:18, NEB).

Not only Jesus' words but also his actions give proof of his obedience to the Law, which was the mark of Judaism. In reading Mark's Gospel, we find that Jesus accepted the Jewish laws related to uncleanness. When he cured the leper (cf. Mark 1:40-44), he completed the healing activity by telling the restored man to have his health officially verified by the priest. Jesus prescribed: "Go and show yourself to the priest, and make the offering laid down by Moses for your cleansing; that will certify the cure" (Mark 1:44, NEB).

We have mentioned that Jesus observed the sabbath, attended the synagogue, studied the Scriptures, and fulfilled the Torah. Because we rarely visualize the person of Jesus as an orthodox Jew, it is worth noting the seriousness with which Jesus affirmed his religious tradition. We all recall the times when the sick begged to at least touch the edge of his cloak (Matthew 14:36). In the special case of the woman who had suffered with severe bleeding for twelve years, she came up behind Jesus and "touched the fringe of his garment." This fringe on his garment marked Jesus as a devout Jew. We find the origin of this religious custom in the Old Testament book of Numbers:

> The Lord spoke to Moses, saying: Speak to the Israelite people and instruct them to make for themselves fringes on the corners of their garments throughout the generations; let them attach a cord of blue to the fringe at each corner. That shall be your fringe; look at it and recall all the commandments of the Lord and observe them, so that you do not follow your heart and eyes in your lustful urge. Thus you shall be reminded to observe all My commandments and to be holy to your God. I the Lord am your God, who brought you out of the land of Egypt to be your God: I, the Lord your God" (Numbers 15:37-41).[1]

Jesus was greatly influenced by the institutions of the Judaism

[1] *The Torah* (Philadelphia: The Jewish Publication Society of America, 1962), pp. 276-277.

of his day. Gerald R. Cragg speaks for our own experiences when he writes:

> We all know how largely we are influenced by the institutions through which we pass, and even when we react against them we still remain their product. . . . These human institutions, imperfect though they may be, are the means by which most of the great things in our intellectual and spiritual experience become our own.[2]

We commonly recognize the part that tradition plays in the makeup of personality. We recognize the traits in the son that are like the father. But if the son is only a replica of the senior, then junior lacks authenticity. To be real, a human has to be an original self.

Tradition helps a person *find* himself (we pattern ourselves after others), but innovation helps a person *be* himself. If one's innovation carries no trace of tradition, we commonly say, "What's he trying to be?" or "Have you ever seen anything like that?" If an individual displays only tradition and no novelty, then we are apt to say, "Stop acting like somebody else. Try to be yourself."

Jesus not only affirmed his religious tradition, but he also innovated, and thereby demonstrated his authenticity. The crowds who heard him recognized that ". . . unlike their own teachers he taught with a note of authority" (Matthew 7:28, NEB).

To be authentic, the individual *cannot* be an exact replica of his elders. Innovation as well as tradition goes into character formation. This is true both for personality growth and cultural development. The social and political institutions of our day carry on many inherited distinctions from the past; but if these groups and movements are to be relevant *in the present,* they must break forth in new modes.

John D. Rockefeller III, who is by definition a member of the establishment, said in a speech he made upon receiving the annual award of the Society for the Family of Man in New York City in 1968,

> The church is what we have made it. Its dilemma is that while its mission should be the righting of wrongs and the active pursuit of the great Judeo-Christian values, we have instead made it for the most part a force for the status quo.
>
> By and large, we are much more conservative as elders of the church than

[2] Gerald R. Cragg, *The Interpreter's Bible,* ed. George A. Buttrick (Nashville: Abingdon Press, 1954), vol. 9, pp. 538-539.

we are as parents. The minister who would remain a minister all too often must please a conservative laity, those who support the church financially. The result is that the church loses some of the finest members of the younger generation.[3]

Jesus not only affirmed tradition; he also broke with it. This was a critical point in Jesus' career. We must ask why a person who affirmed in so many ways his great religious tradition broke with it.

Jesus not only shaped his life on the witness of God in the past, but he also acted in the faith that God is at work in the present.

Jesus recognized, as we must, that every religious ceremony and prescribed act was intended originally to express a spiritual purpose. As long as these religious customs do that, the activities deserve to be reverenced. But when these traditional religious customs fail in their intended purpose to express God's spirit, then they must be replaced by new and living forms of expression.

As William Barrett wrote in *Irrational Man*, "A tradition is kept alive only [by a radical rethinking], not by mechanical and idle parroting of the formulae it has bequeathed to the present."[4]

It is quite clear that Jesus saw a difference between the weightier matters of justice, mercy, and faithfulness and the lighter duties of tithes and ceremonial washings. This distinction revolutionized the Judaism of his day. For example, the devout Jew practiced hand washing before meals. This was an act of consecration, not of cleanliness. The first-century Jew knew nothing of germs and hygiene. He did know that every meal was an occasion both for thanksgiving and religious fellowship. In time the principle involved in thanking God for food and fellowship became a ceremonious cleansing. The careful Pharisee made binding upon himself the washing ritual that was first prescribed for priests in Leviticus 22:6.

Jesus and his followers protested this new interpretation by ignoring the rule, for they saw that it placed a hardship upon the ordinary working people who had little leisure for observing such niceties. As one commentator put it: "There

[3] John D. Rockefeller 3rd, "In Praise of Young Revolutionaries," *Saturday Review*, December 14, 1968, p. 20.
[4] William Barrett, *Irrational Man* (Garden City, New York: Doubleday & Company, Inc., Anchor Books, 1962), p. 110.

66

can be no doubt that Jesus showed a pronounced indifference to questions of ceremonial cleanness." [5]

Contrast this with Halford Luccock's description of this scene:

These Jerusalem scribes, evidently an investigating committee, and the local Pharisees, who had acted as spies, saw the *little* things. They never saw the *big* things. . . . They were interested in pots and pans, in scourings, in the minute details. . . . Their eyes were blind to everything except what threatened their traditions, their vested interest, their authority, and their prestige.[6]

The question which comes to us is this: Do we ever approach issues in the same way as the Pharisees approached Jesus, with our minds made up, so that we never really examine these serious questions at all?

John D. Rockefeller III, who cannot be characterized as revolutionary, said:

. . . children learn much more from what their parents do than from what they say. Many young people state that while their parents talk about love, integrity, freedom, and fair play, their actions are heavily oriented toward materialistic security, comfort, and status. They repeatedly point out that they are not rejecting their parents themselves, but rather what they see as the hyprocrisy of their parents' double-standard approach to important social values.[7]

In June of 1969 the valedictorian for the Harvard Law School said:

I have asked many of my classmates what they wanted me to say in this address. "Talk with them about hypocrisy," most of them said. "Tell them they have broken the best heads in the country, embittered the most creative minds and turned off their most talented scholars. Tell them they have destroyed our confidence and lost our respect. Tell them that, as they use the phrase, 'Law and Order' is merely a substitute for reason and an alternative to justice." [8]

Younger persons are trying to inform their elders that the conflict is real, and it cannot be explained away. The dis-

[5] B. Harvie Branscomb, *The Gospel of Mark*, in *The Moffatt New Testament Commentary* (New York: Harper and Row, Publishers, n.d.) , p. 125.

[6] Halford E. Luccock, *The Interpreter's Bible*, ed. George A. Buttrick (Nashville: Abingdon Press, 1954) , vol. 7, p. 747.

[7] Rockefeller, *op. cit.*

[8] Sanks, Robert R., ed., *Student Recognition Day Workbook* (Nashville: Division of Higher Education, Board of Education, The United Methodist Church, 1969) .

affection among youth involves more than a few radicals. As adults, we have urged visions of a democratic society upon them since their earliest years in grade school. Now we ask them to curb their desires for a society which provides economic equality and social justice. We have encouraged them to dream of brotherhood, and now we suggest that they abandon those hopes. We have commended idealism as the marks of heroes, but now we ask our youth to go slowly.

If our young people rebel against our cautious attitudes, it is because they were listening when we taught them what is right. As one young campus leader said, "It is unthinkable to abandon principle because we are threatened or to compromise our ideals because we are oppressed."

As we have examined the Markan text, we have seen that for Jesus the Law, which included the Ten Commandments and Deuteronomy, was binding. It had been given to mankind by God. But Jesus rejected the tradition which the religious lawyers had added to the Torah. Even within the Law itself, he regarded the spirit as more important than the letter, and some matters more important than others. Jesus was not afraid to innovate within the tradition of the Law itself, for Jesus was conscious that men may come to know God's will by being open to human needs.

Jesus stood in the great tradition that came from Mount Sinai to Mount Zion. But in order to heed man's pressing problems, he was ready to break with tradition. Just as man was not made for the sabbath, so man was not meant to be broken upon hard-nosed tradition. Rather, tradition must yield to human need. One must pay a price whether he bears with tradition or breaks with tradition. Many times the price is life or death. Life dictated solely on traditional grounds is a form of death and eventually brings actual death to a society. The party of the Sadducees was very traditional, and it died when the temple was destroyed in A.D. 70.

The Pharisees were a little more flexible, more adaptable; they tempered the tradition. They learned from the hard lessons forced upon them by prophetic figures like Jesus and Paul and even their own teachers, such as Gamaliel. So the Pharisees survived the fall of Jerusalem and were the forebears of present-day Judaism.

As we know from the book of Acts, the first-century Christians had two major wings, the conservatives and the progressives. The conservative group was called the Jerusalem church and was led by Jesus' own brother, James. The progressive element was led by the apostle Paul.

The conservative faction disappeared with the fall of Jerusalem, but the innovators, under Paul, went on to change the world. How radical Paul's group must have appeared to James and his followers in Jerusalem! Paul did not require the new converts to undergo circumcision! They were not made to follow the dietary laws. They did not even come under the dictate of the Torah. What a radical faith those early Christians preached!

As you read Acts, you can see the struggle between tradition and innovation. As you read Paul's letters, you can see his inner struggle as he tried to move his fellow Jews from their old tradition. "How great is my sorrow, how endless the pain in my heart for my people, my own flesh and blood!" (Romans 9:2, TEV).

The price to pay is stagnation and decline if we do not innovate. If we do introduce new elements, the price often is pain and anguish, for there are times when innovations no longer tolerate a gradual approach.

Some years ago I served a congregation which had benefited greatly from the generosity of a particular donor. At about the turn of the century he had amassed a considerable fortune by selling American housewives a very good bar of soap. It was a black soap. Then some bright fellows down in Cincinnati came up with a household soap that not only had a snappy slogan, "99 and 44/100 percent pure," but also the soap was white. The new white soap drove the old black soap out of the market.

What place was there for buggy manufacturers and harness makers when the automobile was introduced? What place was left for steam locomotives after the diesel engine was built? What place was there for great movie studios, the "star" system, and vast theater chains after television sets were mass-produced?

Some changes are so innovative that they drive old customs from the scene. What place is left for our international policy of supporting military dictatorships in Latin America and Southeast Asia when the mass of people in those countries are pressing for land reform? What place is left for policies that depend on repression and force when populations, particularly youthful populations, are mobile and free to move about? How ironic that the United States, once the haven of the oppressed, is now the exporter of conscientious young men who flee to Canada and Sweden. What place is there for authoritarian forms of governing societies and families when knowledge and education are widespread and loyalty can no longer be coerced but must be freely gained and freely given?

Ernest F. Scott has described our condition: "The problem of the world today, amid widespread bewilderment, is to relate on ever-new levels the originality of a creative person and the tested experience that speaks through tradition." [9]

This crisis which Jesus experienced in his lifetime first helps us to look for God's purposes in the tradition that has come down to us. Second, it helps us to look for God's will in the needs of persons and societies in the present. We are not to be afraid to break with tradition. And third, this crisis points to the importance of looking for God's direction in the possibilities yet to unfold in the future. God, who was present at the Creation and whose power and faithfulness toward men merited the loyalty of our forefathers continues to work in history today. Indeed, the Christian hope in the future is that God is already at work making ready all the vast possibilities which await mankind. He is not only Alpha, beginning, but also Omega, the close and completion.

To bear with tradition? To break with tradition? This is our contemporary problem. Jesus shows us that the process of bearing and breaking with tradition is part of the work of being God's people. God is not only part of the tradition handed down from the past, but he is also part of the dynamic new tradition which you and I are creating as we serve him in the present time.

[9] Ernest F. Scott, *The Interpreter's Bible*, ed. George A. Buttrick (Nashville: Abingdon Press, 1954), vol. 11, p. 107.

8. HOUSE OF ISRAEL ALONE?
Matthew 15:21-28

An authentic crisis in Jesus' life arose when a pagan woman confronted him. She wanted health for her tormented daughter. His first response was unsatisfactory to her. She insisted on gaining his help. How Jesus resolved his own dilemma may demonstrate needed truths for our own situations. Jesus faced right up to the question, "How exclusive is my religion to be?" In our modern experience we may discover what limits, if any, there should be to tolerance.

The problems Jesus brought to this encounter require investigation. This first area of study could be headed "Confronted by Crisis." The actual resolution of the crisis and the significance of Jesus' decision, "Converted by Compassion," makes up the second part of this exploration. The third section deals with "The Consequences of Communion."

The high-pressured appeal of this distraught mother created a real crisis for Jesus. He had just come from what he might have assumed to be the central crisis of his career. He had broken radically with the tradition of the Pharisees. This had been a painful decision, for he counted many of the Pharisees as friends. The teachers in the synagogue at Nazareth who introduced Jesus to the Law, the Prophets, the Psalms, and the other writings were themselves members of the party of the Pharisees. Jesus had broken completely with the Pharisees just before he set out through the foreign territory of Tyre. Some commentators suggest that it was Jesus' controversy with the Pharisees over what really constituted clean and unclean which led Jesus to withdraw from his home territory for a while.

This foreign-speaking mother may have caught Jesus off guard. If he was looking forward to a time of retreat and reflection, the demands of this worried mother were ill-timed.

We ourselves have experienced the bad timing of events. Just when we think we have resolved some great matter at much emotional expense, almost immediately there follows another equally anxiety-filled test. A young mother had moved a thousand miles from her parents' home when she was informed that she must undergo surgery. So in a strange city she went through the most serious medical operation of her lifetime.

71

She was recovering at home when the telephone rang bringing the saddening message of the death of her aged father. Sometimes the pressure of a crisis is succeeded by anxiety of added critical events, which in turn are followed by a new crisis event. It is not altogether uncommon for persons to be faced by this wavelike series of intensive crises. In this instance Jesus was still sorting out the tremendous consequences of his altercation with the Pharisees when a strange woman rushed to him and asked frantically for his help. Strangely enough, humanly enough, Jesus balked at this demand.

Though Jesus' response sounds queer to modern ears, he reacted just as any Jew might and as any Pharisee would. Even though he had burned the bridge of clean and unclean behind him, he still had not worked out all the consequences of his action. He replied, "I have been sent only to the lost sheep of the people of Israel" (Matthew 15:24, TEV). Jesus' response was natural enough. He made the old familiar response even though his situation was utterly new. The newness resulted from his action of breaking with the Pharisees.

Prior to Jesus' decision to break with his tradition, ignoring the foreigner may have been fitting. Jesus, as did every God-fearing Jew, shared intensely in the faith that through Abraham God had chosen Israel as his special instrument to save mankind. Earlier, Matthew records that "Jesus sent these twelve men out with the following instructions: 'Do not go to any Gentile territory or any Samaritan towns. Go, instead, to the lost sheep of the people of Israel'" (Matthew 10:5, 6, TEV).

The consequences of our decisions are never simple nor are they easily apparent to us. This was also Jesus' real life experience. Though it had been traumatic, Jesus' break with the Pharisees did not conclude the matter. He had forced his way through to a new understanding of God's intention for mankind, but he still had to find out for himself just what the limits of the Eternal purpose were.

How free of limitations was God's love? Did God's redeeming care reach out to include only the outcasts within Judaism? Was it possible that God's provision was to be stretched far enough to take in Gentile outcasts as well?

It is not strange that Jesus' mind should be blocked at this point. The Canaanite woman was asking him to throw overboard an enormous heritage. This is plainly visible in Jesus' crude expression: "It is not right to take the children's bread

72

and throw it to the dogs" (Matthew 15:26, NEB). Embarrassed Christian commentators have suggested that Jesus meant this as a joking illustration in order to teach his disciples. Others have suggested that the word "dogs" may really mean "puppies." Jesus may have been repeating a proverb lodged in the recesses of his mind from his childhood, for the words are brutish and harsh. The alternate suggestion offered here is that the unfeeling and rude expression erupted from the deep psyche of Jesus and came tumbling out past the lips of this normally sensitive man. It is not too radical to suggest that Jesus himself was the victim here of that ailment he so skillfully had diagnosed in the Pharisees just a short while before. Jesus himself was the product of religious instruction offered by devout Jews. His years of preparation to be a son of the Law must have filled him full of the widely accepted understandings of his day, and these commonly held ideas included prejudices. We know from other writings that many rabbis designated the heathen as dogs.[1] Why could not some of the most rigorously held assumptions of his instructors rub off on Jesus?

The early church waged a fierce struggle to assert the very real humanity of Jesus against heretics who falsely claimed that Jesus only *appeared* to be human. It was essential that Jesus possess actual human nature if he was to be God's anointed. Christ was God's act reconciling the world precisely because the Divine humbly took up the heavy tasks of a servant. Such a burden included the prejudicial suppositions of the human species with whom he identified himself.

The true nature of Christ's divinity was boldly made visible in this struggle with the weight of the past. His oneness with God was validated when he broke with all tradition that would set limits on God's liberating love. God chose "to be made flesh." A handicap of incarnation is that a person can be infleshed only in a man who is bound by the limits of his age. The Gospels give ample evidence of how Jesus conquered the barriers that blinded his contemporaries. For instance, Jesus had a more open attitude toward children and women than many of his generation.

What is the significance of this event in Jesus' life? Here Jesus dramatically illustrates the dynamics of how God's truth does break into human history.

[1] Cf. George A. Buttrick, ed., *The Interpreter's Bible* (Nashville: Abingdon Press, 1954), vol. 7, p. 442.

We have assumed that his response was just as Matthew recorded it. Such a response would not be unusual to any pious man of that date. However, we have examined only part of the story.

We need also to examine Jesus' background as a man of Galilee. His home province of Galilee was known as the "circle of the Gentiles" (Matthew 4:15; Isaiah 9:1).[2] We may presume that the region acquired this name because it was Jewish territory which was surrounded by foreign nations. The New Testament scholar Dr. Frederick Grant has observed that "the outlook of a Jewish boy growing to manhood in this region, surrounded by Gentiles, and in contact with foreigners from all parts of the world, was necessarily different from that of a citizen of Jerusalem or of any town in Judea."[3]

The fact that Jesus was Galilean allows us to surmise that he may have been more sensitive to God's intention regarding the Gentiles than we have supposed thus far. Jesus was well aware of the example of Old Testament prophets who "did their thing" among the Gentiles. Jesus' words to his hometown congregation when they were pressuring him to do at home what he had accomplished in Capernaum are interesting. Jesus said: "It is true that there were many widows in Israel during the time of Elijah, when there was no rain for three and a half years and there was a great famine throughout the whole land. Yet Elijah was not sent to a single one of them, but only to a widow of Zarephath, in the territory of Sidon" (Luke 4:25-26, TEV). Did these words intrude upon Jesus' conscious memory as he faced this Canaanite mother in Tyre, just about five miles south of Sidon? Perhaps Jesus suddenly recalled his earlier words to the Nazareth audience: "And there were many lepers in Israel during the time of the prophet Elisha; yet not one of them was made clean, but only Naaman the Syrian" (Luke 4:27, TEV). We cannot know what crossed Jesus' mind as the impatient mother insisted that he do something for her greatly troubled daughter.

---

[2] "Galilee" means "circle" or "region"; and *Galilee of the Gentiles* originally meant "region of non-Jews." See Sherman E. Johnson, *The Interpreter's Bible,* ed. George A. Buttrick (Nashville: Abingdon Press, 1954), vol. 7, p. 274.

[3] Frederick C. Grant, "Jesus Christ," *The Interpreter's Dictionary of the Bible,* ed. George A. Buttrick (Nashville: Abingdon Press, 1962), vol. E-J, p. 877.

Didn't Jesus have trouble enough? The whole political and religious apparatus of the Pharisees was turned against him. His disciples were very anxious about attracting any more attention to themselves right at this difficult time. They may have tried already to send her away. They were exasperated with her conduct. This much the Scripture states plainly enough. But the persistence of the concerned mother helped Jesus break out of the box of religious prejudice.

As the worried mother appealed to Jesus to restore health to her afflicted daughter, Jesus obviously was moved by the force of her maternal love. Jesus himself lacked nothing in wittiness, and we have noted the effectiveness of his humorous repartee. Jesus was jolted out of his physical weariness by the woman's sharp wit. His lame response to her insistent request was, "It is not fair to take the children's bread." This evidences that his concern was still for the disenfranchised of Israel.

Her quick response was respectful but to the point: "That is true, sir . . . but even the dogs eat the leftovers that fall from their master's table" (Matthew 15:27, TEV). What a clever thrust on her part! If she had only partially held Jesus' attention earlier, she now had gained all of it. Her sense of humor drew him into her immediate situation. He saw in all its fullness the deep love she had for her daughter. Her daughter's pain was assumed by the mother as her very own. Jesus could feel the mother's hurt. The care God showered upon his children was evident in this mother's concern for her child. Yes indeed, such tender faith was not to go unrewarded.

The compassion of the mother drew Jesus' love forth. He could no longer remain unmoved by the mother's pain. Jesus' words were warm and admiring: " 'You are a woman of great faith! What you want will be done for you.' And at that very moment her daughter was healed" (Matthew 15:28, TEV).

The Gospel account closes there with the encounter completed. However, I feel that Jesus may himself have experienced a sense of new health and fresh vigor out of this run-in with the persistent pagan parent. The mother gained what she intended from her meeting with Jesus. For Jesus this was only the beginning of a radical new way of understanding God's plan for mankind.

Jesus experienced a very real meeting with the Gentile mother. They had taken part in an event common to both. Anguish, pain, humor, and awareness were all shared by the two. Such

75

acts of sharing constitute the essence of communion. We know of only the major consequence of this act of communion. For the Syro-Phoenician woman, her beloved daughter was healed. What were the possible consequences in Jesus' own case? His horizons seemed to have been enlarged. God's urgent compassion was no longer restricted solely to Israel. His view of the kingdom was broader. Luke records Jesus as saying: "People will come from the east and the west, from the north and the south, and sit at the table in the Kingdom of God" (Luke 13:29, TEV). Jesus had opened up the possibility of extending his ministry to include the Gentile outsiders as well as the Jewish castaways.

This awareness of a place for the foreigner in God's kingdom is beautifully set forth in Jesus' illustrative story of the helpful Samaritan (Luke 10:25-37). Jesus used this story as the example when he was asked, "Who is my neighbor?" The despised heathen was the one who risked being robbed himself and personally provided for the expensive needs of the injured man. The finest example of a neighbor that came to Jesus' mind was a member of a despised people. Here certainly was an enlarged vision of how God intended to populate his kingdom.

A similar note of ecumenical citizenship is sounded in Jesus' description of the cosmic court in which the Son of Man, as King and Judge, will render ultimate judgment upon all human affairs (Matthew 25:31-46). All the nations of the earth will be called before this conclusive court session. Judgment will not be based on who enjoyed whom for a forefather, but rather on how each ministered to his neighbor's need. What a broad standard, what a humane scale of values! Not religious regulations nor national considerations but deeds of mercy count on that final testing day.

The modern problems related to tolerance are conditioned by current attitudes. It is popular to assume that any religion is all right as long as you believe in something. This is to confuse tolerance with a "know-nothing" religious attitude. Tolerance actually requires some sense of communion with the other. Jesus exercised tolerance toward the Canaanite mother, and she reciprocated tolerance because each shared something with the other. If either of them had been indifferent, that one would have ignored the other.

For a Protestant not to know anything about modern Catholicism is not tolerance, but ignorance and indifference. For a

Christian to be unaware of the practices and beliefs of modern Judaism is not tolerance, but benign bigotry. True tolerance requires some measure of participation in affirming the other. To appreciate some persons or groups is impossible unless you share something authentic with them. Ignorance and indifference contribute to suspicion and bigotry. Tolerance makes community possible.

Headline events in not too distant years have provided tragic proof of the high cost of intolerance. Moslems of Bangladesh and West Pakistan have paid a high toll in human life for their intolerance. This has also been true of the militant minded among the Protestants and Catholics of Northern Ireland. These tragic events replay in the late twentieth century some of the horror experienced in earlier centuries when intolerant men laid waste to entire continents in their effort to impose their bigoted ideologies.

Contrasted to the tragic consequences of intolerance, the practice of toleration produces happy results indeed. The headlines are not as big, but there are no lists of dead either. It may be as simple as a Jewish synagogue presenting an award to a Protestant minister, as did happen in Westfield, New Jersey. Or the practice of tolerance may be inviting a Protestant to teach on a Catholic theological faculty, as is happening across the nation.

When Protestants were attempting to bring up to date the King James Version of the English Bible, they found the need for a Jewish scholar. So today the Revised Standard Version is not only an immensely popular edition of the Holy Scriptures, but it stands as tangible proof of the benefits of tolerance.

Not too long ago the United Methodist Church sponsored a project to allow young pastors, less than five years out of seminary, to engage in intensive small-group experiences spaced out over two years. The design of this pilot project included a series of retreats. In Oregon the Young Pastors' Seminar included Lutherans, Episcopalians, Baptists, Disciples, United Church members, as well as Methodists. At one of their retreats the young pastors were accompanied by their wives. On Saturday they "rapped" with a Catholic priest, who served as a campus minister at the state university. On Sunday morning the priest offered mass in a small parish nearby. Prior to the mass, he was instructing the little congregation in some of the hymns to be sung in the actual worship when in walked the

77

entire group of young pastors and their wives. So the priest wittily announced, "I've invited some 'ringers' to help us sing." So, two score of young Protestant clerical families, attending a retreat sponsored by Methodists, helped the Catholic congregation to sing a hymn written by Martin Luther. This is happy fruit of toleration, indeed.

Jesus apparently found difficulty in working through this question of the tolerance of his faith. Certainly he recognized that he could expect only increased opposition from the leading churchmen of his day. He risked considerable misunderstanding. In our day the risk lies in allowing tolerance to deteriorate into indifference. The Christian who slides into indifference not only loses his own faith but denies the authenticity of the faith of others as well. To engage in toleration requires a grasp of one's own beliefs and an openness to appreciating the beliefs of others. Jesus, whose life is the anchor point of the Christian community, struggled through to a more adequate awareness of God's divine purpose for human history. The modern church has ample opportunity to write new chapters on developing religious toleration.

9. WHEN A SIGN WAS DEMANDED
Mark 8:11-21; Matthew 12:39-41

A crisis came in Jesus' life when the Pharisees challenged him: "You're supposed to be God's man, so now prove it. Work a miracle!" In what almost amounted to a replay of the temptations, they pressured Jesus to satisfy the popular expectations of wondrous signs. "Give us proof, man!" They dared Jesus to whip up a miracle in order to comform to the crowd's image of a man of God.

It is difficult enough to be put on the defensive with, "So you're supposed to be somebody. Well, show me." The Pharisees' contention was more than just another psychological game perverse people play. For Jesus to yield to their demand would have the effect of denying his entire mission and message. A similar dare had drawn an angry response from an earlier religious leader who yielded to the impulse to "show the scoffers." Moses struck the rock, and water gushed out. This reflex action in the heat of dispute robbed Moses of personally entering into the promised land (Numbers 20:12; 27:14; Deuteronomy 34).

Today many persons demand the same kind of assurance that the Pharisees wanted Jesus to produce. On what terms does God make real his presence to man? The arrogant challenge of the Pharisees was rejected by Jesus. Their hostile contentions prompted Jesus to warn his disciples about the leaven of the Pharisees. The only wondrous proof Jesus would promise his detractors was the sign of the prophet Jonah.

The study of three Scripture verses may assist us in understanding how Jesus handled this crisis: Mark 8:12 contains the demand for a miracle; in Mark 8:15 Jesus warned that the leaven of the Pharisees was hazardous to spiritual health; an analysis of Matthew 12:39, 41 may reveal what the sign of Jonah meant to Jesus.

Mark recounts that when Jesus heard what the Pharisees wanted him to do, "Jesus gave a deep groan and said: 'Why do the people of this day ask for a miracle? No, I tell you! No such proof will be given this people!'" (Mark 8:12, TEV). You can sense the deep pain Jesus felt when these religious leaders came to him insisting: "Grant us a wonder!" Apparently the Pharisees and Herodians were content to accept signs and wonders as the credentials for a spokesman of God. Is this not to mistake the magical for true evidence of the divine action? Theirs was a common enough error because men do tend to seek God in the abnormalities of life. Jesus experienced God's self-disclosure differently. He found God showing himself to man through the normal processes by which life is created and sustained.

The Pharisees were asking for instant proof of the cheapest sort, a demonstration on their terms. If Jesus had given in to their claims, he would have failed his calling. The faithless are content with something sensational; the faithful trust enough to try to do the will of God without spectacular evidence. Jesus described the only confirmation the loyal servant requires: "Whoever is willing to do what God wants will know whether what I teach comes from God or whether I speak on my own authority" (John 7:17, TEV).

Jesus resisted the demands for an extraordinary sign because such marvels cannot be taken as guarantees of God's action. Jesus had already said that he would have nothing to do with magic when he spurned the temptation to dive from the temple towers to test God (Matthew 4:1-11).

Jesus did heal many persons of their diseases, but this was not done to show off some supernatural power. His compassion led him to help the sick. Jesus effectively freed personalities from the demonic powers which possessed them. He restored health to sick bodies. Such healing gave evidence of his care for people. It was not done in order to convert the faithless. Compassion rather than sensationalism moved Jesus to make men whole.

What did such "mighty works" mean? We can today reject the common concept of a miracle as an unexplainable event which conflicts with the laws of nature. This definition of a miracle as a violation of natural laws was formulated in the heyday of Newton's mechanical model of the universe. Twentieth-century science no longer pretends that nature is forever tied down to mechanical laws. The universe once again is open to an appreciation as old as St. Augustine. This Christian philosopher thought that since it is God who creates and controls the universe, all of nature is miraculous, although men are more familiar with certain miracles than with others.

Ever notice children whenever their pet has pups? Or their first experience when the household cat has her kittens? What a wondrous time! As we grow older, some of this anticipation and sense of wonder at new life beginnings seems to be educated out of us. Because we now have seen diagrams illustrating the process, we seem to feel that we know all about it. Our modern sophistication has robbed us of the sensitivity we once enjoyed, which allowed us to take delight in the "millions of miracles" that happen every day.

But Jesus was spared our modern hang-ups on miracles versus natural causes. He realized that he was privileged to be able to help people out of deep troubles. From the very start of his prophetic ministry Jesus blended together his telling of God's kingdom with his doing of marvelous acts. The Gospels chiefly report his restoring of health to sick bodies and releasing persons from demonic bondage. Jesus counted heavily on prayer to do this important work. The authority of his own personal conviction helped rid people of diabolical influences.

Jesus saw such deeds of mercy not as magical signs and mysterious wonders but as the "mighty works" of God. These were evidences of the emerging reality of God's kingly rule. Jesus did not resort to these exorcisms and healings as proof of his authority. That he was able to set bodies right and liberate personalities was proof to Jesus that God's rule was taking hold. ". . . by means of God's power that I drive out demons, which proves that the Kingdom of God has already come to you" (Luke 11:20, TEV).

These wondrous deeds demonstrated that God was making his real presence count in human affairs. In Judaism's past, the events of the Exodus under Moses and the Exile under Ezekiel had shown God's active participation. Israel's miraculous deliverance from Egypt and Judah's marvelous restoration after the captive years in Babylon provided concrete evidence that God did rule history and did control the destinies of men and nations.

In the same way, Jesus saw the events of his time making visible the mighty works of God. Jesus claimed no supernatural powers for himself. These healing acts arose from a source beyond his personal possession, for God's immense power was not a commodity to be controlled by any other being. Such awesome capability to restore and renovate belonged solely to the majesty of God. Jesus intuitively recognized what Moses and modern men have discovered through tragic experience. God is generous in making his awesome power available to any man in need. However, God is jealous of anyone claiming

81

personal ownership over the tremendous resources that belong to the Creator alone. Jesus knew God as the ground and source of his healing efforts.

It is difficult for modern persons to appreciate the awesome experience of God. We lack the dimension of dynamic awareness which Jesus knew. One possible reason for such spiritual anemia is that our age is afflicted with an extreme case of self-confidence. Our writers boast of mankind as having come of age, though our urban slums, rural junk heaps, and swollen military budgets give more evidence of a cultural senility than a social maturity. We are also infected with an insensitivity to our own moral depravity. We have managed to convince ourselves that evil does not exist and man no longer sins. In the face of the longest and cruelest military engagement in modern times (we no longer even call it war) while drug addiction short-circuits young lives into horrible, premature deaths, we brag about man being his own god.

We need to be delivered from these demonic bosses of cultural pride in order to recover our awareness of God's ruling majesty. The Hebrew prophets were aware that God is always present. It is man whose spiritual nerve endings have become insensitive to the holiness of the Creator. The example of Jesus helps us, as modern thinkers, to recover the truth that everything in the universe including natural history and human history were from the first, and still remain, the creation of God.

Ours is a modern, secular problem. Jesus actually replied to an ancient, religious one. Men have often sought for divine power in terrifying acts and awe-inspiring feats of wonder. Jesus rejected this appeal because he recognized that such notions were akin to magic. The God he knew was not interested in manipulating man nor in being manipulated by man. Israel's God did not depend upon sensational feats or horrifying wizardry to relate to man. When the Pharisees and Herodians asked that God perform acts to their satisfaction, this suggestion bordered on blasphemy.

Jesus was so enthusiastic about the very strong evidence of God's work, which he continued to find daily, that he was visibly disturbed by these contentions for sensational proof. Wasn't God setting persons free from their ancient physical and mental tyrannies? Jesus did not look upon himself as a performer of wonders and a worker of miracles. He made no claims that he produced these much needed healings by him-

82

self. He had known times and places where God's power could not break through. He could recall the experience he had in his hometown. "There he could not do any miracle, beyond laying his hands on a few sick people and curing them. He was astonished at their lack of faith" (Mark 6:5, 6, Moffatt).

What cures Jesus had been able to effect in his ministry depended on the faith of the individual and God's answer to prayer. Jesus interpreted such returns to health and sanity as significant evidence of God's power. This was proof that the age of the kingdom was dawning. Casting out demonic powers and restoring health to broken bodies gave evidence to the fact that the power of evil had been broken. God's universal rule was about to be established. Jesus saw these "mighty works" as tangible evidence of the new messianic age. God was introducing his reign.

The Pharisees' disputations fell wide of their target. With the telltale marks of God's activity bursting forth all about them, they wanted to have some of the old-fashioned kind of superstition and sorcery. They could not see the real thing because they so much wanted some of that old-time magic.

This kind of hankering for the outdated tricks of sacral alchemists still takes place. Not too long ago, a local church "imported" a group of high school athletes to "give their testimonials." These teenagers used some of the time-worn jargon, such as "Jesus laid a burden on my heart. . . ." This was an alien language to the high school from which the youngsters came. Where had they learned such secret passwords? What was taking place was a parroting of phrases taught them. Why had this congregation invited this group? Perhaps because they still performed the kinds of wonders which reminded some old-timers of the marvels of an earlier, revivalistic period. These young ballplayers confessed that they had been "living a life of sin" (at ages as early as eleven and twelve) before they were "saved" by this wonderful athletes' group.

The tragedy of this "charade for church elders" was compounded in that these searchers for signs and wonders had overlooked their own big group of young people. Without the glamour so many find in athletics, the youth of that congregation were involved in band, orchestra, choir, forensics, drama, student council, scholastic honoraries, and Boy Scouts. More importantly, perhaps, the church youth group had organized a teenage drop-in center where town young people could find a quiet place for conversation or study. This center was started at an important point in the life of that small city when drug addiction was becoming a problem among high school youth. The church youth group sensed a need for a "neutral" place to meet. They cleared an understanding with the police; the young people were to take the responsibility and promised "no drugs" while the police promised "no busts."

That same church youth group had followed through upon its denomination's statements regarding a need for penal reform. The youth board organized a visit by the young people to the county jail. Then the juvenile case worker was invited to meet with the church school youth class. These meetings were followed by group interviews with a county commissioner and, later, the judge of the juvenile court. Such plans and arrangements were started by young persons themselves. The fact that such civic responsibilities were shouldered by Christian young people was entirely overlooked by a group of adults who sought certain verbal signals they had always associated with proof of God's work.

The kind of proof demanded by the Pharisees and Herodians would have qualified someone to be a worker of miracles. Jesus' interest was in something more than psychic spectaculars. The teacher from Nazareth was so wide awake to the wondrous doings of God that he actually groaned out loud when both religious and political leaders ignored the sure evidences of God's action and blindly asked for magic and wizardry. In the first instance, Jesus answered negatively, "Why . . . ask for a miracle? . . . No such proof will be given!" (Mark 8:12, TEV).

Shortly after this dialogue about miraculous signs, Jesus warned his disciples: ". . . be on your guard against the yeast of the Pharisees and the yeast of Herod" (Mark 8:15, TEV). What was dangerous about the Pharisees and the Herodians? They were a strange alliance. As a strict religious group, the Pharisees usually did not associate with the Herodians. The party of Herod did plenty of business with the Roman overlords and so copied many of the heathen customs and ideas of their military masters. As a rule, the Pharisee would avoid association with the lesser, political breed of men. However, expediency often begets strange alliances. These two groups were so afraid of Jesus as a threat to the religious and political establishment that the ruling party and the religious elite ganged up against the Galilean.

Jesus was a threat to the political dynasty and the puritanical clique. If men were to accept Jesus' teaching that God's kingdom is now present, such believers might alter their civic loyalties and change their religious commitments. This unsettled the already shaky political and ecclesiastical establishment. Jesus' mission and message seemed to be revolutionary. To the men in power his actions and teachings appeared to be seditious and heretical.

Jesus' own disciples failed to appreciate his warning about the yeast of the Pharisees and the Herodians. According to Mark's account, they mistook him to mean that they had failed to bring extra bread (Mark 8:14, 16). However, Jesus' thoughts were still on the previous episode. What was the yeast of the Pharisees and of the Herodians?

Recognizing that our views may well be as far from the mark as was the disciples' response, we may still venture an opinion. The yeast of the Pharisees may have been spiritual pride while the yeast of the Herodians was a desire for earthly power. Let's consider each group in order.

The Pharisees placed their trust in tradition. Theirs was a religious society of men who separated themselves from those less zealous in doctrinal matters. They represented the backbone of the Jewish nation. They were deeply devout and utterly sincere. Modern usage does them an injustice when we use the word Pharisaic to describe a hypocrite. The Pharisee was trying to do what every dedicated churchgoer tries to do today. He tries to be good and "keep the faith" as best he knows how.

Why, then, beware of the yeast of the Pharisees? What happens when people preserve religion just for the sake of preserving it? "It's a good thing to do. Everybody ought to go to church regularly. It makes you feel good inside." We have heard that argument. We have used that argument. But religion for its own sake is not enough. ". . . ever since I was young I have obeyed all these commandments" (Mark 10:20, TEV), the rich man said to Jesus. Jesus looked at him "with love" Mark notes. It is good to keep the commandments. But this is not enough, for Jesus replied to the rich young man, "You need only one thing. Go and sell all you have and give the money to the poor, . . . then come and follow me" (Mark 10:21, TEV). Commitment to one's spiritual heritage is necessary and very worthwhile. To be religious is basic, but conscientious piety alone is not enough. To consider it sufficient just to be creedally orthodox represents the yeast of the Pharisees.

This warning needs to be heeded. Such yeast marks much of man's religious efforts. Throughout history, men have fallen victim to the ill effects of such spiritual yeast. The first of the Crusades was preached in order to save the Holy City of Jerusalem from the infidels. In time, and not a very long time in terms of Europe's history, crusades were being waged against the pope's political enemies. The papacy often ate too well of the yeast of spiritual pride. But lesser Christians than the pope have suffered the same ailment.

Later in Europe, the yeast of the Pharisees took on a different form. Sören Kierkegaard warned his fellow Christians of the ills of Christendom. They denounced him, in turn, and scorned him because he failed to realize how privileged he was to live in Denmark where the culture was Christian, where the state was Christian, where philosophy was Christian, and where all education was Christian; in short, that society had become hooked on the yeast of the Pharisees.

Such yeastiness allowed some persons to set themselves up as better than their brethren, and this action led to tragic consequences. Need we be reminded of the superior spiritual sorts who drove Roger Williams off into the wild country during a New England winter? Shall we recall the witchcraft trials of Salem, Massachusetts? No, the puffed-up pride of phony piety which afflicts men was not limited to any special place or single historic period. The historian of religion can find traces of the yeast of assumed spiritual superiority in almost every land, at almost any time. Each one of us may well heed Jesus' warning. It may be our condition which he has diagnosed.

If spiritual snobbery is the yeast of the Pharisees, what is the yeast of the Herodians, Herod's political followers? The Herodians suffered from a rather modern virus, that of the love of earthly power. They accommodated themselves to political and military power. If power required that they play up to the Romans, they made that accommodation. No compromise was too much in order to gain power. The yeast of the Herodians allows men to suppress all concern for decency and justice in order to gain and hold power.

In the summer of 1971, the *New York Times* angered both Republican and Democratic political leaders by publishing certain historical documents which dealt with the start of American involvement in Vietnam. Quoting from top-secret Pentagon documents, *Times'* reporters told of a nation's leaders deliberately misleading its people. James Reston commented early after the first stories broke. Speaking of the official documents, Reston wrote: "One of the many extraordinary things in this collection is how seldom anybody in the Kennedy or Johnson administrations ever seems to have questioned the moral basis of the American war effort." [1]

One of the tragic consequences of "the yeast of Herod" is that once a person acquires a burning thirst for power, it is difficult to maintain a balanced life. All values and all other duties must give way to the demands of the drive toward power. Herod's drive for power was marked by many murders and mass violence.

Reinhold Niebuhr made a great contribution to Christian thought by describing this drive to dominate others. He analyzed the ways in which men plan, scheme, and connive to gain mastery over other men, particularly over masses of men. The "Christian realism" about which Niebuhr wrote was much like the practical good sense used by the American founding fathers. Recognizing the abuses of power, the framers of the Constitution set up three separate branches of government: the legislative, the executive, and the judiciary. This separation of powers recognized that the concentration of powers is dangerous to any healthy society.

Jesus warned his disciples to watch out for "the yeast of Herod." In modern times, military power seems to have been inflated by Herod's yeast. Great nations have succumbed to the military mentality which sees might in terms of fire-power and measures success with the "kill-ratio." The leaven of Herod induces democratic nations to help arm dictatorial nations with military equipment far beyond protective needs or capacity to buy. So the poor of such nations protest, and the military oligarchy uses the dearly purchased planes and tanks against their own protesting people. The international policy of great nations is terribly complex indeed, but it was no modern political scientist in a modern "think tank" who put his finger on the fatal flaw. It was a prophet of God (who was too late for the age of prophets and too early still for the world of "men

[1] James Reston, "McNamara Papers Prove Truth First Casualty of War," *Oregonian* (Portland), June 16, 1971, p. 43.

come of age") who cautioned, ". . . be on your guard against the yeast of the Pharisees and the yeast of Herod" (Mark 8:15, TEV).

The challenge that he prove himself by showing some "sign from heaven" was answered by Jesus, "Why does this generation ask for a sign? I tell you this: no sign shall be given to this generation" (Mark 8:12, NEB). Elsewhere, Matthew records another occasion when some Pharisees and Sadducees wanted to trap Jesus: ". . . so they asked him to perform a miracle for them, to show God's approval" (Matthew 16:1, TEV). "His answer was: 'It is a wicked generation that asks for a sign; and the only sign that will be given it is the sign of Jonah'" (Matthew 16:2-4, NEB).

What Jesus may have meant by his question, "Why does this generation ask for a sign?" (Mark 8:12), is made more obvious in Matthew's account of a "wicked generation." In the widespread thinking of the people of that time, the age of the Messiah was to be marked by perversion and evil. The wickedness of the times was added proof for Jesus that he and his critics were living in the time of the Messiah's coming. Messianic signals were there: the gross sinful acts of Herod and his court; the cheating and conniving of the quisling sort of Jew who oppressed his fellow countrymen to win favor with the Roman overlords; and the debasement of the moral fiber of Judaism by the introduction of depraved Hellenistic practices. Paul's report is accurate historically:

They boast of their wisdom, but they have made fools of themselves, exchanging the splendour of immortal God for an image shaped like mortal man, even for images like birds, beasts, and creeping things.

. . . They are filled with every kind of injustice, mischief, rapacity, and malice; they are one mass of envy, murder, rivalry, treachery, and malevolence; whisperers and scandal-mongers, hateful to God, insolent, arrogant, and boastful; they invent new kinds of mischief, they show no loyalty to parents, no conscience, no fidelity to their plighted word; they are without natural affection and without pity (Romans 1:22, 23, 29-31, NEB).

This is not an exaggerated picture of events in the Roman Empire in Paul's day. It also is a fitting description of the intrigues of the palace crowd in Jerusalem. It really was a "wicked generation." So Jesus saw the prodigality and monstrous evil as further evidence that his was the messianic age. To such a self-deluding people, too blind to see past their sin-glazed eyes, Jesus could promise only "the sign of Jonah."

He answered: "It is a wicked, godless generation that asks for a sign; and the only sign that will be given it is the sign of the prophet Jonah. . . . At the Judgement, when this generation is on trial, the men of Nineveh will appear against it and ensure its condemnation, for they repented at the preaching of Jonah; and what is here is greater than Jonah" (Matthew 12:39, 41, NEB).

The Old Testament Book of Jonah is really a short story. In just about two pages tucked between Obadiah and Micah, you will find the reluctant prophet. Even the slim story seems to be hiding, which is not surprising when you consider the hero of the story. Jonah was a loser of the worse sort. He tried to lose, and the Lord wouldn't let him. Then Jonah peevishly called the Almighty to task for not letting him fail. Why would Jonah want so badly to fail?

Jonah did not believe in the mission God wanted him to undertake. Jonah wanted it literally to be a "mission impossible." Certainly Jonah did not believe even in its possibility. When the mission did succeed, Jonah acted almost as if God had double-crossed him.

Why such bitter feelings? God had commissioned Jonah to go and denounce the great city of Nineveh for its wickedness (Jonah 1:1, 2). Jonah immediately boarded a ship headed in the opposite direction. He meant to go to Tarshish to be "out of the reach of the Lord." But after a storm, followed by a whale of an experience, Jonah started off again, this time in the right direction.

When Jonah did reach Nineveh, the city was every bit as bad as the Lord had pictured it. Jonah couldn't see much hope for these people. He made a halfhearted effort to preach the word of judgment. Really, halfhearted is too strong a word. This sorry excuse of a prophet only managed to go a third of the way across the big city before he threw away the punch line. Is this too harsh a description? Here is the way the Bible has it: "[Jonah] began by going a day's journey into the city, a vast city, three days' journey across, and then proclaimed: 'In forty days Nineveh shall be overthrown!'" (Jonah 3:4, 5, NEB).

Asking Jonah to preach the word of judgment that might save the chief city of his nation's mortal enemies, the Assyrians, was like asking an ultra-right-wing American politician preacher to carry the word to Moscow in order to save Communism. In such a case, the committed anti-Communist might just head for the Antarctic, which is what Jonah did. God finally turned him around and, despite the prophet's hesitant performance, the multitudes of wicked heathen actually heard him.

Then the most amazing thing happened. Even with such limited input, there were tremendous results!

> The people of Nineveh believed God's word. They ordered a public fast and put on sackcloth, high and low alike. When the news reached the king of Nineveh he rose from his throne, stripped off his robes of state, put on sackcloth and sat in ashes" (Jonah 3:5, 6, NEB).

"Now there is a sign for you," said Jesus. Jonah was hardly a dynamic preacher; he planned no long-drawn-out campaign, and no months were spent in preparing the city for a mass crusade. An inept prophet made a feeble attempt in the face of massive immorality. But the people, high and low, heard the judging word of God and repented right away. The people of Nineveh paid close attention to the faltering words of the stranger, and they took it as a sign that morally they stood condemned. So the king decreed a time of fasting and praying. ". . . call on God with all [your] might," he instructed his subjects. "Let every man abandon his wicked ways and his habitual violence. It may be that God will repent and turn away from his anger: and so we shall not perish" (Jonah 3:8, 9, NEB).

What was the sign of Jonah? It was evidence of the inability of the moral people to take seriously God's concern for the immoral and the lost. The Ninevites heard God's judgment. The godless people were ready to plead for God's mercy. What about the godly folk whom Jonah represented? These good people were so filled up with their spiritual pride that they really could not believe God, not even when they were asked to do something. They could not take God's word for real even when God did something right in front of their eyes.

Very much like Jonah, they could only pout and complain that God was being unfair. "Those dirty heathen don't deserve to be forgiven. Such wicked pagans ought to be wiped right off the face of the earth." Jonah was so mad that God had been merciful with the immoral aliens of Nineveh that Jonah actually prayed: "And now, Lord, take my life: I should be better dead than alive" (Jonah 4:3, NEB).

The sign of Jonah was there for all to see. They had only to look at Jesus' own ministry. Who was Zacchaeus? Just a notorious chiseler whose graft made him a despised enemy of the people. Yet Jesus dined with him and forgave him. What of Matthew? Was he not just another notorious tax collector? Still, Jesus included him among his twelve closest associates. How about that alien, the Roman centurion? Weren't the Jewish people being flattened under the heavy military boots of just such career officers? Does Jesus deny that God's power is effective in the life of a commander of conquering, foreign troops? Or take the case of the Syro-Phoenician woman, another barbarian. Doesn't Jesus acknowledge that she, too, is entitled to God's providential care?

Jesus deliberately carried his liberating ministry to the poor and the outcast. He insisted that these wretched of the earth were entitled to first-class citizenship in God's kingdom. While the publicans and sinners were left out of the more orderly systems of religions by the orthodox leaders, Jesus declared that God has a warm welcome prepared for the repentant prodigal. For those looking for a sign, there was plenty of evidence of Jonah's sign.

Jesus' contemporaries refused to see the work of God as it plainly happened all about them. Contrast their stubborn unawareness with the pagan people of Nineveh. Even though surrounded by heathen darkness, they acted promptly when the evidence was placed before them. Jesus assured them that the sign of Jonah was certainly available to his own generation.

We live in times when men fail to recognize the signs of God's redeeming action. Sometimes sincere men are tempted to smite the rock in order that men might know that God is still at the work of creating and sustaining life. If the Pharisees were denied assurance through miracles, why do we today persist in expecting biblical faith to magically cure all the world's ills? Is it not important to begin by first rejecting the unusual and abnormal as "proof" of God's healing and reconciling efforts? Then we might try to be more sensitive to the possibility that normal channels might disclose the Father.

We could also work at cleansing ourselves of the leaven of spiritual pride and the yeast of arrogant power. With these two huge tasks underway, we might then look about for the signs of Jonah. Where is the word of judgment being expressed? What should we be repenting of, right now? Who are the citizens of Nineveh in our own time who, while not of our own faith, are acting as men of faith should? Religious men continue to make demands for a sign. The answer still remains, "No sign will be given, except Jonah's." If we begin to look around us, we may begin to recognize a few such signals.

10. WHEN JESUS COULD NOT AVOID DISSENT
Mark 10:2-9

As have many of his followers, Jesus faced a personal crisis in regard to dissent from the established order. As a faithful son of the Law, it was no small decision for him to disagree with the religious leaders on a basic matter of faith. What can we learn from Jesus' experience when he faced a situation where dissent could no longer be avoided?

Before going on to examine Jesus' response, a few general statements regarding dissent may help our understanding. The word "dissent" means disagreement with the majority opinion; dissent may express either the withholding of agreement or an open indication of disagreement.

Dissent is vital to the Christian faith, essential to our freedom, and an important component of human community. A true democracy is not afraid of dissent and protest. Indeed, many political scientists see in dissent an important safety valve. For a democracy to work it is essential that there be lines of communication between the persons who govern and the people who are governed. Normally the political parties and special interest groups serve as channels of communication. Unfortunately such lines of contact are often broken because so few people are politically motivated. How many of us, for instance, are involved actively in the processes of the political parties of our nation? Often the citizens with the most intense grievances are least able to attract the attention of governmental officials. Thus, ill feeling smolders and is harbored until sometimes such built-up hostility explodes into violence.

The founding fathers of America understood this essential requirement that it must be possible for a citizen to express his thoughts. The First Amendment guarantees the right of all citizens to freely state their opinions. The assumption of the Bill of Rights is that dissent is peaceful even though painful to those who wish both elected power and popular support.

Privilege bears a price. Americans are a privileged people with basic rights guaranteed by the Constitution. All law and order is based on this. When you examine the price tag of freedom closely, you will find that one of the costs of liberty is to be tolerant of dissent as well as to be ready to engage in dissent.

92

Reasonable and informed dissent are always needed in a working democracy.

Now let us examine the question of dissent from the perspective of Jesus' experience. In the first place, dissent is a principle of faith. Open disagreement with the majority position is in the Christian tradition. This may strike you as a bold claim, but we only need to turn to Mark 10:2-9 to discover it to be a true claim. Jesus was a dissenter from the very tradition in which he had been reared. As did the Hebrew prophets before him, Jesus differed sharply with and dissented vigorously from the established religion of his day. In this position, Jesus stood in the tradition of Amos, Jeremiah, and John the Baptist.

This passage on God's intention for man and woman is usually referred to for an understanding of what Jesus taught about marriage. This same Scripture passage can be examined from another perspective. What can it tell us of how Jesus expressed his dissent? If you look with care at this historic incident, you will notice that Jesus made a break with the fundamental law of the land. Jesus dared to criticize the law-giver, Moses. Jesus harshly accused his listeners: "It's because you are so hard to teach that Moses was forced to grant that law" (cf. Mark 10:5). Jesus viewed the existing religious-legal code on divorce as an accommodation made to a perverse people. So we are looking, not at the issue of divorce, but at how Jesus handled the *law* on which the divorce practice was based.

To appreciate the emotional response of the Pharisees, imagine someone saying to members of one of our Rod and Gun Clubs that it is "because of the wickedness of your hearts that the founding fathers wrote into the Constitution the clause granting citizens the right to bear arms." The Pharisees responded to Jesus at this same gut-level.

On what basis did Jesus attack the Law of Moses? Jesus appealed to a higher law. He appealed to a moral principle already present in the act of creation. Ever since creation, men have resorted to a similar appeal to a more fundamental law that stands behind the written codes of men. The American founding fathers appealed similarly to such a law when they wrote: "We hold these truths to be self-evident . . ." (Declaration of Independence). When is dissent appropriate? Whenever it is essential to transfer the discussion to a higher realm. In the debate on divorce, Jesus appealed to the purposes of God as the basis of his dissent.

The German reformer Martin Luther appealed to the fundamental law found in the Bible when he dissented from the man-made laws of Christendom. In the early nineteenth century, the English social reformer William Wilberforce appealed to fundamental laws applicable to all humanity when he attacked the governmental-commercial complex which grew rich from the transport and sale of human slaves.

Dissent from established custom and man-made laws is in the Christian tradition. Dissent is a basic ingredient of faith. Dissent is an essential component of what the late Paul Tillich called the Protestant principle. This is the principle of evaluation, criticism, and correction which is essential to any social movement or organization if it is to remain healthy and vital.

The example of Jesus himself, in his dissent from his own first-century Judaism, encourages us to see dissent as belonging within our Christian heritage.

In the second place, dissent is a principle of freedom. As such it is part and parcel of our Christian tradition. The list of dissenters in religious history reads like a roll call of saints and martyrs: John Bunyan in England, Roger Williams in the American colonies, Martin Luther King, Jr., in more recent times. Each was a prophet with a role in man's search for justice.

I am a Baptist serving as chaplain at a college founded by Baptists. A short while ago some high school students invited me to speak to an assembly of theirs. When they urged me: "Now really say something . . .," I tried to do so. I spoke on "Deepen the Revolution." Now that word "revolution" really makes some people choke up. Some of the letters and conversations since then have revealed that many adults are uptight about the word "revolution." We, as adults, do need to find ways to be more relaxed in light of the information revealed in a poll of college freshmen published in *Time* magazine. *Time* reported: "One out of every three freshmen said that he believes the U.S. needs some sort of revolution, and one out of five described himself as either a radical or a revolutionary." [1]

Now if that information does not add to our discomfort, this additional finding may. Of the college freshmen interviewed, "A substantial minority believe that U.S. society is more repressive today than it was two years ago, and a majority think that a period of greater repression lies ahead." [2]

[1] "Spirit of '73," *Time,* October 10, 1969, p. 49.
[2] *Ibid.*

94

Have you noticed signs of increasing repression? Do you find your freedom of inquiry curbed? Is your liberty to express yourself more restricted? Or are these young freshmen just imagining it all?

Older citizens sometimes take a defensive position while citizens of a newer generation take an offensive posture when discussing what younger militants perceive to be "political trials." Without deciding for either side, can we examine some such events in order to sharpen our senses about possible dangers to our civil liberties?

For example, in 1969, eight persons were brought to trial in Chicago's Federal Court on charges which had grown out of events of the previous summer. When the Democratic Convention met in Chicago in the summer of 1968, demonstrations turned into serious clashes between the police and the demonstrators. Congress responded swiftly and passed a law barring interstate travel in order to minimize the disorder.

The eight accused were brought to trial under this new law. *Life* magazine reported that an Illinois director of the Civil Liberties Union called this "the most important political trial in the history of the United States." [3] The case brought into focus such matters as freedom of speech, freedom of assembly, freedom to travel, and protection against unreasonable search and seizure.

In describing the Chicago case, reporter Furlong writes: "It seems as if all the prosecution has to do to convict the defendants is prove they crossed state lines and discussed the organization of disorder with somebody somewhere somehow for some reason. The penalty is up to 10 years in jail and a $20,000 fine." [4]

If the law is so loosely formed, it would appear that a minister could not deliver a sermon on dissent in a church in his neighboring state for fear that he might be violating a federal statute.

The trial of the Chicago 8, according to the *Life* magazine report, was the "wrong test of the wrong law in the wrong place at the wrong time." [5]

As a nation the United States has had to subject itself to some very difficult self-examinations in recent years. The tragedy

---

[3] William Barry Furlong, "The Straights vs. the Chicago 8," *Life*, October 10, 1969, p. 28 D.
[4] *Ibid.*, p. 30.
[5] *Ibid.*

of American involvement in Vietnam has been compounded by substantiated cases of brutality. First, the public was shocked by accusations that the Green Berets had murdered a Vietnamese employee who apparently was discovered to be spying for both sides. Because the man was suspected to be a double agent, he was allegedly murdered. American legal and political leaders, such as the former associate justice of the Supreme Court, Arthur Goldberg, raised their voices to protest. The allegation that members of the American military had executed a foreign national without a trial violated the military code. Specifically Article 106 of the Uniform Code of Military Justice requires a trial and conviction before an appropriate tribunal even for alleged spies not in uniform caught behind the defensive lines.

Hardly had the American public been able to adjust itself to the barbarities unveiled in accusations leveled in the Green Beret case when atrocities with even greater consequences were unveiled in the obscure village named "My Lai." Articles 93 and 118 of the same Code of Military Justice make it a crime for an American serviceman to murder or even to practice cruelty toward "any person subject to his orders." The United States also subscribes to the Geneva Conventions, which impose similar restrictions.

As the Vietnamese war has wound down, Americans of conscience have had to face the harsh reality that the troops our tax dollars have equipped have used that equipment to murder infants, children, women, and old men at point-blank range. In *Life* magazine Arthur Goldberg referred primarily to the earlier Green Beret incident, but his statement is an indictment of all such revelations of criminality committed under the conditions of war.

> . . . the situation in Vietnam cannot justify us as a nation now, for the first time in our history, to tolerate—more, to legitimate—the cold-blooded murder of individuals wholly under the control of our troops. . . . individual American soldiers may not take it upon themselves, away from the battlefield, to serve as prosecutor, judge and executioner.[6]

Does it not seem incongruous that a government which is ready to prosecute demonstrators in Chicago and peace marchers in Washington in order to maintain law and order shows a leniency toward its own military troops that murder innocent citizens of another country?

[6] Arthur Goldberg, "Guest Privilege," *Life*, vol. 67, no. 16 (October 17, 1969), p. 30 D.

96

Speaking personally, as a citizen and a Christian, I find this inconsistency in governmental policy an irony I cannot tolerate. I have found it necessary to dissent publicly from such an unfortunate double standard. We cannot operate under one standard of justice in Vietnam and a different standard in our homeland.

But why should I be troubling you with such concerns? Isn't the church supposed to be wrestling with spiritual concerns? Why not let the politicians wrestle with these worldly concerns?

Precisely, my friends, justice, mercy, and righteousness are the concerns that the Bible and the Christian faith are all about. And we as Christian spokesmen must attempt to call our nation into account. But perhaps I have set for myself an impossible task. Perhaps it is too late. Perhaps our consciences are so dulled that we can no longer distinguish between what properly belongs to God and what we owe to the nation.

As church historian C. C. Goen writes in the Baptist journal *Foundations:*

> The fundamental problem, as I see it, is that whereas some 70 percent of Americans are counted on the rolls of our many religious bodies, we are not at all the "Christian" nation we like to think we are, but essentially a secular one. That is to say, our primary values as a people derive not from the Christian gospel but from secular society. The paradox, however, is that most people do not know this, and if someone tells them so, they do not believe it.[7]

In plain words, our congregations are so comfortably housebroken to the American culture that we get along quite well with it and feel no strain between what we do on any Sunday morning and what our nation is doing seven days a week, such as making war in the name of peace. Or as Professor C. C. Goen puts it, "The God confessed by most Americans is a deification of The American Way of Life."[8]

As American military involvement in all parts of the world increased, many religious leaders spoke out against such a militaristic national posture. Church figures encouraged the return to more peaceful methods for pursuing the nation's proclaimed goals. Such efforts for peacemaking were often misinterpreted. Whether it was Catholicism's Cardinal Terrence Cook, or Judaism's Rabbi American Heschel, or the World Council of

[7] C. C. Goen, "The Cultural Captivity of the American Churches," *Foundations,* July-September, 1969, p. 197.

[8] *Ibid.,* p. 200.

Churches' Dr. Eugene Carson Blake, who spoke for peace and against militarism, some political leaders would interpret the peace-seekers' show of dissent as giving aid to the enemy. Such politicians seemed to be asking: "What are religious leaders for except to support the nation's political leadership and get behind the national efforts?"

This apparent nationalistic blind spot is precisely why dissent is so essential to faith and freedom. God will not sit still in any nation's pocket. God will not automatically stand behind every national cause, nor can we as Christians be any less discriminating in our support of our country.

I love this nation dearly. My military record as a young man stands behind my pledge of allegiance, but my primary allegiance will always be to God, who revealed himself in Jesus Christ. I am grateful that the founders of this nation had the wisdom to provide for basic freedoms — of speech, of assembly, of worship. While I have breath, I shall voice my dissent whenever our nation falls short of its high calling.

We began with an examination of Jesus' dissent to the basic Law of Moses. The serious nature of such dissent cannot be overemphasized. Jesus was doing more here than just differing from the interpretations of Pharisees, Sadducees, or scribes. He was calling into question the basic formulation of the Mosaic Code upon which rested the Judaism of that day. He certainly was aware of the radical character of his dissent. His hearers were also alive to his strong statement of fundamental difference.

Thus far we have said that first, dissent is part and parcel of faith. Second, dissent is essential to freedom. Third, and finally, dissent is a necessary part of fellowship. Dissent must be provided for if we are to be human in a community of shared interest. Dissent belongs to congregational life and to family life. Does this sound strange, even contradictory? Some feel that fellowship, community, congregation, and family are relationships where we do not have nor do we need dissent. However, I propose that a social condition where all must think alike, behave uniformly, and stick rigidly to a given code of thought or conduct is not fellowship nor community nor a family. I would suggest that the current problem referred to as the "generation gap" is largely created by intolerance to dissident feelings, thoughts, and actions. The lack of tolerance knows no age limitations.

To be different, to be free to express differing views, to be tolerated, yes, to be loved when we express a dissenting opinion — these are the experiences that build community. Love means more than just agreeing with those who agree with you. Differing personalities and the different points of view are what make a fellowship — not the sameness, not the loyalty to a party line, nor the conformity to cant and shibboleth.

If you and I are to be part of any fellowship — a living part — your humanness and my humanness must be affirmed. Such affirmation must be realistic enough to recognize that you and I, to be human, must express our individual lives, think our own individual ideas, and speak our own words.

In short, community is *not* sameness and conformity, but community is individual difference and corporate variation.

Where there are differences, we must allow room for dissent.

The Hebrew prophets paid a price for the privilege of dissent; Jesus knew and paid the price; the Reformers rose up and fought for the right to dissent; the American founding fathers included the right to dissent in the basic law of the land. Are you and I to be content with anything less?

11. WHEN JESUS WAS QUESTIONED ABOUT TAXES
Luke 20:20-26

Taxes concern most of us more than just once a year. True, Americans do pay out their income taxes on or before April 15 each year. You and I also pay a gasoline tax every time we fill up the tank, another tax when we purchase a theater ticket, yet another tax when we buy some cosmetics or jewelry.

Taxes are not only a heavy expense, but they are also a constant reminder that there is a power in our society that compels our financial support whether or not we care to contribute voluntarily. Follow the flow of tax money, and you will learn much about the realities of any society, any civilization.

It was just such a real life issue which confronted Jesus when some unfriendly types tried to corner him with a potentially dangerous question.

In his record, Luke rewrites Mark's description of some of the Pharisees and some of the Herodians who came to interrogate Jesus. Luke calls them secret agents or spies. He also says right out loud what Mark only hints at, namely, that these hired character-assassins were looking for a pretext in order to hand Jesus over to the "authority and jurisdiction of the governor." What meaning is there in the scoundrels' question about paying taxes to Roman authorities?

Three steps mark our study of this event in the life of Jesus: First, *the trap* set for him in the question about taxes; then *the debt* every citizen owes to the country in which he lives; and third, *the allegiance* which binds the lives of all faithful men and women.

The history behind the tax known as the tribute to Caesar is interesting and important to this situation. It was an annual tax collected by the Romans. The levy was introduced when Archelaus was deposed. He was the incompetent son of Herod the Great and the last of the Jewish puppet princes of Judea. When Roman procurators in A.D. 6 took over the administration, they instituted a survey of the resources of the country for the purpose of taxation. This aroused intense resentment among the Jewish population. A revolt broke out with its leaders declaring that the taxation was a "direct introduction of slavery." The Romans suppressed the revolt, but the popular resentment against this tax never stopped.

The levy was particularly unpopular to a militant party known as the Zealots. Their slogan was "No king but God." To have the profile of the deified emperor on the coin added to the humiliation and injury, for it clearly violated the commandment central to the faith of Judaism, "Thou shalt not make unto thee any graven images" (Exodus 20:4, KJV).

Mark, in his Gospel, makes note of the unholy alliance that waited upon Jesus. The coalition of the Pharisees and the Herodians was a most unnatural one. Normally, the aims of the two groups were different and opposed to each other. The Pharisees were a strict Jewish sect who desired to see God's rule extended to the whole of life and over all the world. They felt that Jesus was too unorthodox in religious matters. The Herodians, on the other hand, were very political. They wanted to see the party of Herod firmly entrenched in power. So they favored the Romans and were courting the political leaders in Rome for support. The Herodians saw Jesus as a dangerous political foe.

These strange bedfellows devised a clever trap for Jesus. If Jesus said, "Yes, pay the tax," he would alienate the nationalists and lose the confidence of the people; if he said, "No, don't pay the tribute to Caesar," he was open to the charge of treason.

The snare set for Jesus came in the form of a question: "Is it right for us to pay taxes to Caesar or not?" (Luke 20:22, Phillips). The pitfall presented to modern Christians comes in the form of a direct statement: "Don't mix politics and religion."

The churches today are paying a heavy price because clergymen and denominational leadership have spoken out on the plight of the poor, the rights of the minority, and our involvement as a nation in Vietnam. Now an unholy alliance of the very religious and the very political are interrogating Christian leaders: "Is it right that you have mixed politics and religion? Why don't you fellows stay with preaching the gospel and stop meddling in such political matters as war and peace! Leave that to the military. Let the congressional committees worry about how we spend our national budget. Besides, didn't we put God into the pledge of allegiance to our flag? Isn't 'In God We Trust' on every dollar? Get back to preaching, son, and leave politicking to us."

When Harry Truman was president, his pastor spoke out against the presidential proposal to send an ambassador to Rome. The president refused to return to his church. Time has vindicated the pastor. Today Roman Catholic scholars are among those who emphasize the fact that the Vatican is a source of spiritual leadership rather than an earthly principality.

More recently our presidents have tried to isolate themselves from unpopular preachments. The president from the Lone Star state discovered the power of the present-day pulpit. On one occasion he very carefully tried to woo the nation to his position on the undeclared war he had escalated in Vietnam. Shortly after his nationwide address, he attended a church. The young pastor laid aside his prepared text and bared the agonies of conscience which were troubling him as well as much of America. The well-planned propaganda coup of the president was dealt a death blow by the candor and conviction of one conscience-stricken pastor.

America has seen presidents whose imaginations were fired by trips abroad to nations where the pomp of royalty still survives. President Nixon attempted to transpose some of his experiences in royal capitals onto the American scene. For instance, he tried to spruce up the White House guard, but the effects were ludicrous. The first public display of their new finery reminded some observers of a high school production of a Gilbert and Sullivan operetta.

Dressing White House police in white jackets, brass buttons, and plastic caps may seem silly, but serious is the initiation of another custom of royalty, the effort of heads of state to have their own private chapels and their own personal chaplains. The nation's most celebrated evangelist served as personal chaplain to our nation's highest elected official, and each Sunday on which President Nixon was in the White House, there was a well-publicized religious service held there with specially selected speakers. What was less publicized was the important fact that the President successfully isolated himself from any religious opinion that would be critical of any presidential political policy. He had his religion without any of the prophetic, critical elements that might upset him. The most clever way to try to avoid the judgment that religion should bring to bear upon man's political affairs is *not* to outlaw religion, but actually to *sponsor* religious events.

In a democracy no church deserves any favors from the

government. As Christians we ask for no special privilege. Our only right is to be heard, and our only instrument is that of persuasion.

But in order to persuade we need an occasion to be heard — no special hearing, just the regular occasions of public worship. To seal oneself off in a private chapel may be the prerogative of royal personage, but an American president who is truly democratic, not to say truly religious, will not deliberately isolate himself from the voice of conscience. The White House may attempt to avoid the persuasions of the pulpit through the devices of a selected invitation list, a captive congregation, and a carefully selected speaker. But an insulated president attending private worship in his own isolated chapel is neither practicing true Christian worship nor honoring the authentic tradition of American democracy. The highest office of the land must not be isolated from the issues that trouble a democratic people.

Taxes not only define the flow of power, but they also describe a debt owed by the citizen. In ancient times the sign of kingship was the sovereign's authority to issue currency. In these modern times the ability of the government to regulate the flow of currency shows where the real power lies.

In the past, rulers gained from this right to issue currency the consequent right to impose taxes. To accept and use the currency of the realm is to obligate oneself to the government which issued the bills and coinage. We recognize this in modern times, for if a Canadian moves to the United States, or if someone moves from one of the states to a Canadian province, he not only uses the coinage of his new residency, but he is liable also to the taxes imposed there.

If a man lives in a particular state, he cannot divorce himself from it. In Jesus' day the Roman coins had Caesar's profile imprinted on them. They belonged to Caesar, and he had a right to demand them. The coins were regarded as his property, but Jesus pointed out that certain debts and duties belong to God. God has put his imprint upon man, and God can call in his coinage, the image of God that is carried by the human person.

The more honest a man is, the better citizen he is. Yet in the life of the Christian, God has the final word.

We know well the debt which we, as citizens, owe to our nation. Allow me a personal reference. My father and mother immigrated to America to flee the harsh economic and political conditions of the Austro-Hungarian Empire. This once great power had exhausted her wealth and ablest sons on countless petty wars for more than a half century. In these United States my parents found safety and dignity. My parents have three sons. I served in Europe in the Second World War. My brother served on the fighting front in Korea. Our youngest brother served in the army during these recent times of the Vietnamese conflict.

This is one way of paying our debt to our nation — to give up our sons, our husbands, our fathers. Is this the only way? Does this complete our responsibility as citizens and Christians?

As a citizen I have not exhausted my indebtedness by serving in my country's wars. As a Christian citizen, I must also call my government to task. As I have watched the television screen and have seen civilian Vietnamese farm workers floating dead on the river with their hands tied behind their backs, my conscience has cried out. I want to know if my tax dollar supports that kind of activity.

How far do you go in obeying the state rather than the Christian conscience? This question has been raised by many Christians. In more recent times the young German theologian Dietrich Bonhoeffer faced it. He had little help from Martin Luther's teaching that the two, church and state, were separate kingdoms. What if the state violated fundamental Christian morality, as when Hitler's regime systematically murdered millions of German citizens just because they were Jews? Bonhoeffer felt that in Christian conscience he must oppose his own government. So he worked in the underground church. But even then he was not relieved of the painful act of wrestling with his conscience. To Bonhoeffer, a Christian pacifist, came a frightful dilemma: He was asked to have a part in planning the assassination of the demonic Nazi leader, Adolf Hitler. If he refused, he would be guilty of allowing the assembly-line murders of innocent Jews to continue; if he took part in the planning, he would be guilty of the death of one man, his nation's ruler. Either way he was guilty of murder.

Now in no way am I suggesting that as Americans we are at the stage, nor even near the stage, of being forced to go underground. Our democratic institutions, particularly our judicial system, remain strong and virile. So it is not rebellion that is suggested. What I am saying is that the issue of our debt to our nation is every bit as serious for us as it was for Bonhoeffer.

What is my responsibility as a Christian when I read that U.S. military officials, without authorization from Congress, secretly gave 150 million dollars worth of military equipment to Nationalist China? What is my responsibility when I read that U.S. infantrymen declared under oath that they were instructed by their superiors in Vietnam "not to take prisoners." This means that it was the practice to kill captured enemy soldiers, an outrageous violation of human decency and international conventions of war.[1]

Jesus left the decision to his listeners. What is our debt to Caesar? What is our debt to God?

Dr. G. H. C. Macgregor is surely right in thinking that the basic truth underlying Paul's words is that "the principle of ordered government for the protection of justice is divinely ordained" and not that "any particular government, which happens to be in power, is so because God Himself has ordained it. . . ."[2]

As E. F. Tittle states:

> It is a serious matter to oppose the State in the name of God, not only because of the personal and social consequences which this may entail, but also because it involves the assumption that one definitely knows what the will of God is. . . . But what is the Christian to do if he is deeply convinced that obedience to the State would be disobedience to God?[3]

As a Christian, I live in the faith that God governs history. What does allegiance to the state require of me as a Christian? What shall I do when obedience to the state means disobedience to God? This is a question of conscience and each of us draws such lines in our own individual ways. But as a community, the church has said and our nation has legally recognized that the state may *not* take what the citizen recognizes as due to God.

When Jesus was confronted with this important question, it had not been much more than ten years since the Roman Senate had voted divine honors to Caesar Augustus at his death.

---

[1] Norman Cousins, "To Those Who Take Freedom Seriously," *Saturday Review*, April 18, 1970, p. 24 f.

[2] G. H. C. Macgregor, *The New Testament Basis of Pacifism* (New York: The Fellowship of Reconciliation, 1936), p. 118.

[3] Ernest Fremont Tittle, *The Gospel According to Luke* (New York: Harper & Row, Publishers, 1951), p. 216.

Temples were being erected to him all over the Empire. Have nothing to do with that, Jesus says. *There is an allegiance which belongs to God alone.*

As Christian citizens we recognize that there is a debt we owe to the state. We affirm that these claims should be met without surrendering our ultimate loyalty which is to God alone.

Jesus suggests that it is quite appropriate for the state to ask back what has its stamp on it, but he surely says that the state may not take for itself what has God's image stamped on it. What that is, his questioners must decide. Even Caesar has God's image stamped on him.[4]

As Chief Justice Charles Evans Hughes wrote, ". . . . freedom of conscience itself implies respect for an innate conviction of paramount duty." "The essence of religion is belief in a relation to God involving duties superior to those arising from any human relation." [5]

What is it that we as Christians have to make as a unique contribution to our nation?

Paul Scherer has answered this question: "There is a kingdom that God brings! To him whom we worship, the offer of the land that we love. For the land that we love, the offer of him whom we worship!" [6]

Wherein is our responsibility? Each one of us must decide our responsibility in the daily exercise of our duties as citizens, as Christians.

[4] Macgregor, *op. cit.*

[5] *United States* v. *Macintosh*, 283 U.S. 605, as quoted in Tittle, *op. cit.*, p. 218.

[6] Paul Scherer, *The Interpreter's Bible*, ed. George A. Buttrick (Nashville: Abingdon Press, 1952), vol. 8, p. 352.

12. WHEN JESUS WAS OFFERED THE USE OF VIOLENCE
Luke 12:54-56; Matthew 26:47-54

Violence continues to sweep across our confused land. One year it is seen in a New York City town house. Another year violence occurs at a state university, or even in the halls of Congress itself. Yet another month violence comes to a California bank. Wherever and whenever — such bombings are tragic tokens of the savagery which threatens to disembowel our nation.

The Weatherman faction of the Students for a Democratic Society includes the most militant elements of the student revolutionary movement. Their rage against the inequities of our inequitable society often crescendoes into destructive lunacy. The Weatherman faction acquired its designation from the lines by Bob Dylan which suggest that we can tell the way the wind blows without having to wait for the weather report.

This poet laureate of young Americans has echoed some of the concern first expressed by Jesus. Jesus directed these remarks against the religious leaders of his day, but from his words we may be able to discover some clues to what is happening in our day. Jesus said to his hearers: "What hypocrites you are! You can look at the earth and sky and tell what it means; why, then can't you interpret the meaning of this present time?" (Cf. Luke 12:56.)

Both Bob Dylan and the Nazarene carpenter argue that the signs of the times are not trick puzzles that only an expert few can understand. No, the signs of the times should be recognizable to all thoughtful and concerned persons. Just as many among us can read the evening skies for the indicators of tomorrow's weather, we ought to be able to recognize what is happening all around us.

What can we tell about our national future from the signs easily readable in any newspaper or viewable on any televised newscast?

The violence we witness daily in our society spells clear danger of a catastrophe of national proportions unless we immediately deal sensibly with the causes as well as the symptoms. First, then, the signs of our times point up the dangers of the way of violence.

In his final moments as a free man, Jesus was offered again the use of violence. The disciple Judas betrayed him. This was Jesus' last chance to escape certain death. Any of us brought up on television drama would leap at his chance to escape into the dark night. Jesus did have the jump on his captors. He could easily have melted into the familiar hills and joined the underground partisans who were preparing to rise up in rebellion against Rome.

Jesus could have gotten away. His disciples knew it. He knew it. So the crisis was real enough. Several of his band were ready to cut their way through the line of temple police who surrounded them. "Shall we strike with our swords, Lord?" some of his disciples asked (Luke 22:49, TEV). Indeed, John's Gospel records Simon Peter as actually lashing out and disfiguring one of the temple servants (John 18:10).

While in the hands of his captors, Jesus was faced with the opportunity to escape. His final chance was almost an instant replay of the third of the temptations. For a moment the old temptor reappeared, "All this I will give you if you kneel down and worship me" (Matthew 4:9, TEV). Again Jesus was tried, not by Satan, but by his own followers who wanted to save him from treachery.

Jesus resisted their tempting offer of escape. "Put your sword back in its place, for all who take the sword will die by the sword" (Matthew 26:52, TEV). When the destructive weapon was drawn, Jesus ordered that it be sheathed. Jesus clearly understood that you cannot win peace by using the sword. Surely a sign we should be able to read is that our military mentality is reducing our nation to rubble.

Ordering the National Guard to Kent State did not bring peace but death. Ordering the state militia into Detroit did not bring law and order but death and destruction. Fifty caliber bullets tore up modern apartments with destructive impact. After the supper dishes were done, a little boy took the garbage out. He was shot dead by a guardsman who reacted to something rustling in the dark.[1]

A great many people have asked why our youth are so radical. Columnist Harriet Van Horne wrote: "For the source of their radicalism we must look to the state of the nation. In the appropriations of Congress you may see the erosion and decay of

[1] From *Report of the National Advisory Commission on Civil Disorders, New York Times* Edition, 1968, p. 68.

democracy. Sixty cents of every tax dollar go for what the young people rightly call 'the economy of death.' " [2]

We have no money for scholarships for needy students. We cannot afford pay raises for underpaid postmen or firemen or policemen or school teachers until they are forced to strike in order to gain an increase. But we do have millions, even billions, for overruns on the cost of military hardware. The army, the navy, and the air force show up with the inflated costs of gross overruns.

Jesus said that "all who take the sword will die by the sword." This is true today. The violence in our society is proof enough that the nation that lives by the sword shall perish by the sword. Any modern nation that bases its national and international policies on the deliberate use of violence will surely beget violence in its own streets. The use of force looses the worst passions of men. By the time a "war of justice" has been concluded, the passion for justice has changed into bitter and violent hatred.

The morning newspaper which came on a particular Memorial Day carried a photograph of the burial stone of a young man. He was born on Pearl Harbor Day of 1944 and died in Vietnam. His all too brief lifetime was bracketed by violence.

Kenneth Keniston, a psychologist at Yale Medical School, interviewed a number of youthful radicals. He writes that the issue of violence with its accompanying fear and anger starts with the earliest memories of these young radicals. ". . . these memories indicate a special sensitivity to the issue of violence — inner and outer — that continues as a central theme in their lives." [3]

The President's Commission on Violence has predicted that the policy of responding to violence by reacting with increased violence is dangerous. Such a repressive pattern is certain to push our urban centers toward a garrisoned city-state burdened by martial law.

Earlier, I mentioned that the National Guard did not restore law and order in Kent or Detroit. Law and order are not a product of police power. Rather, public order depends on law-abiding citizens.

[2] Harriet Van Horne, "Acts of Violence Illuminate Dissatisfaction with Society," *Sunday Oregonian,* March 22, 1970.

[3] Kenneth Keniston, "The Burden of Violence," *Adolescence for Adults* in A Report by Blue Cross, vol. 22, no. 1 (Chicago: Blue Cross Association, 1970), p. 55.

The presence of the militia does not create a lawful social order. If anything, troops provide a totalitarian society. True law and real order come through persons who choose to live in domestic tranquillity.

Harriet Van Horne has caught the frustration felt by many militant young persons. "While Congress closes its ears to the cries of the people for a better life, while bending a slavish knee to the whims and fantasies of the military, the young will go on making demands — and bombs." She warns, "a nation that lacks the machinery for peaceful change will find itself torn apart by violent change." [4] Eric Sevareid reported on television that even at the Pentagon we are beginning to hear voices saying that it is time to put the military genie back into the bottle.

The first sign of our times warns us of the danger present in policies based upon violence. The second sign of our times reveals some possibilities open for the way of reason. Matthew records Jesus as teaching that if you "remember that your brother has something against you, leave your gift there in front of the altar and go at once to make peace with your brother; then come back and offer your gift to God" (Matthew 5:23, 24, TEV). It seems appropriate to recall that sage recommendation. We Americans are estranged from our brothers, both abroad and in our own homeland. We need to make peace with one another. To continue the present state of estrangement is an offense to the Lord of history and is a speedway to destruction.

Today we are faced with the alternatives of violent self-destruction or possible reconciliation through patient, responsible discussion. I trust that our community leaders, university officials, and national figures will speak in tones and actions of reconciliation rather than in authoritarian gestures of disguised violence.

The religious leaders of Jesus' day chose violence. They eliminated Jesus by turning him over to the Romans and accusing him of crimes against the state: treason, sedition, rebellion, and conspiracy to overthrow the government. On such charges Rome executed Jesus.

This was a tragedy for the Jewish nation of the first century. They needed the moderate voices of men like Jesus. The failure to leave room for his prophecies made inevitable the eventual destruction of Jerusalem.

4 Van Horne, *op. cit.*

110

There must be a place in any vital social order for open discussion and reasonable debate. An important change took place in the attitude of the Nixon administration. They listened, for the first time, to the voices of the rebellious young. There was an obvious change in the response of President Nixon to the various peace demonstrations. Early in the Nixon administration, the news media informed the nation that the president had been watching televised sports events while the peace marchers paraded in Washington's streets. However, the springtime rallies following the Kent State incident and Cambodia involvement in 1970, as well as the Vietnam veterans' march in spring of 1971, had the attention of the president along with all of official Washington. Because the administration and congressional leaders were open to the dissenters, the marches were peaceful; and the dialogue and communication necessary to a vital society was possible.

The signs of our times underline the importance of remaining open, of listening seriously, of responding in ways that clearly show that we have heard, and of doing things differently as a result of our listening.

Careful listening is proved by changed behavior. We cannot afford any further hidden acts of violence on the part of the adult generation. When adults modify their behavior, we can expect modified behavior from the young.

President Nixon's action of deliberately ignoring the peaceful marches in the fall of 1969 added directly to the mood of violence in the nation. His behavior was a form of punishment based upon the withholding of favors. We have known for years that it is needlessly cruel for parents to say, "If you do not behave, Mommy won't love you." Adults have tended to withhold society's favors until youth conforms to adult expectations.

Before citizens begin to penalize state universities because of militant students, we need to recall Bernard Shaw's remark that one should always spank his children when in a violent temper. If he doesn't, he misses the only good result which accrues to the spanking: the satisfaction it gives the adult. Rather than spank, we need to support those university presidents who have chosen the way of discussion, of compromise, and of informed debate — not because the young agitators are always right, but because indignant taxpayers also lack the certainty that they are always right. The truth in any human and historical situation seldom lies with any rigid position taken at either extreme.

111

The best way to arrive at truth is to participate in an open exchange of the various perspectives of all concerned.

We need the young as an integrated part of our total society. The noted anthropologist Dr. Margaret Mead has written that our young people today know things about our present life that we cannot possibly know because of the outmoded ways in which we have acquired our knowledge. She compares our present cultural situation to that of immigrants to a new land where the children are more readily teachable. Our society needs this special knowledge of the young if we are to survive.[5]

But the young do not really recognize the significance of what they know except as they talk, study, discuss, and debate with those of us who are their seniors. In short, we need each other if our society is to effectively handle the pressing needs of our times.

In conversing with a group of students, I made some alternate suggestions in regard to present United States policy in Vietnam. One of the students attempted to overwhelm my arguments by saying, "Well, President Nixon knows best." I astonished the student by suggesting that I probably knew as much about the Vietnam situation as did the president. I am sure that the student thought me to be a very arrogant professor. The statement that a common citizen just might have as much useful information as the president of these United States was based upon two private hunches. The first hunch is that the president probably has more information than he can possibly use. This hunch is derived from personal experience.

For many years I had an executive responsibility which attracted to my desk regular reports from over forty city and state offices plus all kinds of national organizations. I have experienced the maddening task of trying to deal with a steady flow of vital information that somehow had to be digested. My responsibility was a hundred times *less* important than the president's is. No doubt you have already moved ahead of the arrogant professor. Probably you are thinking, "But the president of the United States has many assistants. They help him digest all that information." This is true, and that fact provided the basis for my second hunch.

I had a hunch that the president's information is limited to what his assistants tell him. This idea also grows out of

[5] Margaret Mead, "Youth Revolt: The Future Is Now," *Saturday Review,* January 10, 1970.

112

personal experience. In order to cope with the steady flow of vital information, I had an administrative assistant who tried to predigest the volumes of reports. When I came to my desk, there were always three piles: the urgent, the less important, and the least important. But in the process of deciding, my assistant occasionally made mistakes. We both did, and what we may have assumed to be least important turned out to be very important indeed. Remember, my executive responsibility was not one one-hundredth as important as that of the president of the United States. The point is that because of the volumes of input, the chief executive has difficulty sorting out the most important. Often enough the staffs of the *New York Times* and the *Washington Post* do as good a job with the actual facts as do all of the presidential assistants. As President John Kennedy is reported to have said: "I don't think the intelligence reports are all that hot. Some days I get more out of the *New York Times*."

My hunches that day debating with students were confirmed later in a *Time* magazine essay entitled "Does the President Really Know More?" [6] Nearly two years after I first made that statement in public, a reporter from the *Washington Post* confirmed this intuition. It would appear that America's thirty-seventh president rarely watched television except for sporting events and had little time for reading newspapers; so he has depended largely on a daily news summary prepared by a staff of four full-time aides plus part-time helpers, government typists, and duplication clerks to gain his impressions of what was being reported in the press.[7]

What is the point of this argument? First, it is reckless to attribute unreserved wisdom to authority alone, as when uninformed citizens say, "Well, I leave it to the president. He knows best." Such attitudes are appropriate in monarchies and dictatorships rather than in popular democracies. Indeed, this very availability of useful information to almost any interested citizen is the most powerful argument that we actually do live in a vital and free society. However, I am not suggesting that the president of our nation sometimes does not have information and knowledge which is not available to an unknown professor in a little college.

[6] "Does the President Really Know More?" *Time*, May 25, 1970, p. 18.
[7] Don Oberdorfer, "Special Newspaper Gives President Impression of Press —and He's Unhappy," *Oregonian* (Portland), May 16, 1971.

Second, what I am saying is that the health of any vital society requires that both the president of the country and a professor have relatively equal access to all sources of information that bear upon the course and direction of the life of those peoples governed by democratic processes.

All of this is related to our discussion of the need for reasonable dialogue. Just as I am convinced that our youthful campus leaders have need of information sometimes hidden in executive files, I am equally convinced that college presidents and national presidents have need of the dynamic wisdom and contemporary information that only the young themselves can provide to him.

One of the most exciting meetings in the memory of many persons at one college took place in the spring of 1970 right after the Cambodian invasion and the killings of the students at Kent State. At a jointly called session, students and faculty crowded into the student center. They discussed, debated, and agonized over what should be done on a variety of campus and national issues. With a spirit of equality of expression — one man, one voice — young and old struggled through in a most creative fashion to some corporate decisions. The way of reasonable discussion brought some satisfying results to both students and faculty. There was gain in mutual respect as faculty members and students heard one another in responsible dialogue.

We need to listen to the voices of those who differ from us. Such openness to dialogue is urgent in our time. We must pursue the way of responsible discussion if we are to avoid the way of violence.

In a democracy the entire citizenry, not just a part of it, must be informed and deserves to be listened to. Responsible leadership must not hide behind a faceless generalization, such as "the silent majority." Democracy is not run by voiceless and nameless ghosts. Democracy is the open expression of the voice and will of a free people.

Theologically, this process in which truth is discovered through open, frank discussion has been called the work of the Holy Spirit. It is a doctrine which asserts that every single one of us has access to the whole of truth, to the wisdom of God. Not just the man in the pulpit, though he may be especially experienced and educated, but every thoughtful believer in the pew has God-given insights that must be shared with the larger body of believers if God's truth is to be made known.

114

This is why we have church meetings, discussion groups, and small-group meetings. Through free, responsible dialogue, the Holy Spirit may permeate our discussion and God's truth may direct our lives.

In our society, which is threatened by destructive violence and which supposedly is open to the methods of responsible discussion, the Christian community has a larger responsibility: that of demonstrating that we care about people. The hidden violence of our times has caused such injury that many people today are not ready to enter into a meaningful dialogue until they see clearly that there are persons who deeply care about them.

We have noted the dangers of the way of violence and examined the more peaceful way of reasoned discourse. The third sign of our times indicates an urgent need for the demonstration of the way of compassion. Our world obviously needs men and women who really care for other persons.

We have come to take certain qualities about Jesus of Nazareth for granted. It is quite remarkable to note, that in this moment of crisis — the betrayal to the temple authorities — Jesus not only refused the route of violence and escape, but actually his attention was directed to the slave whose ear had been lashed by the awkward swordsman.

The early church fastened its attention upon the miracle of Jesus healing the injured ear. In our self-centered world, I profess to seeing an equally important miracle in the event of Jesus' overcoming his own situation of being arrested and dragged off to some terrible end. Jesus was not so overwhelmed by his own desperate condition that he could not find time to be concerned for the hapless slave whose ear hung torn from his head. Ever since, men who have set their eyes on this person of Jesus have discovered a strength like his own. A modern martyr, Dietrich Bonhoeffer, puzzled over this source of power:

Who am I? They often tell me
I stepped from my cell's confinement
calmly, cheerfully, firmly,
like a squire from his country house. . . .

Who am I? They mock me, these lonely questions of mine.
Whoever I am, Thou knowest, O God, I am thine! [8]

The Academy Award film, *The Midnight Cowboy*, brutally

[8] Dietrich Bonhoeffer, *The Cost of Discipleship* (New York: The Macmillan Company, 1959), p. 15.

portrays the horror experienced by the lonely people who exist in a cruel city. Surviving amidst almost total alienation, the characters inhabit a jungle of passion and brutality where sudden violence compounds the deliberate neglect of personal being. Our first response to this film was deep personal shock. The hatred was too raw, the violence too cruel, the loneliness too much to bear. We wished that the sense of our uneasiness would fade away. As the days passed, the mood of dejection failed to disappear. The tragic loneliness experienced by the Midnight Cowboy stayed with us. Then we ourselves began to make some of the discoveries of Joe Buck, the Midnight Cowboy. He had come to the big city to fleece the suckers; he had himself been taken to the cleaners. Separated from his worldly goods, reduced to a token of his humanity, this lonely creature finally found that he could care for another destitute person.

This man who had never really known authentic compassion discovered what it really means to care for somebody else. Out of this hell of human suffering, the pitiable person of Joe Buck, born loser, discovered that he could care for someone. The very real horror was transformed into a small but real hope.

This is what the Christian church is supposed to be all about. We are a people set in the midst of the world to help others discover what it means to care.

Unfortunately, the church has failed miserably at its God-given task. Quite often we actually contribute to the violence of our times. Frequently we add to the escalation of the fury. We add divine sanction to nationalistic causes. Christians in the past have regarded national goals as divinely given and nationalistic aspirations as sacred duties.

In the film *Midnight Cowboy,* religion is pictured as another of the oppressive forces of a greedy society where everybody is trying to get theirs as quickly and as easily as possible.

Yet Christ calls us to a different task. We are to demonstrate compassion. We are given power to share concern. We are energized to show a more excellent way.

Recently a friend from a congregation I once had served shared some of his personal experiences as a meditation with the board of deacons of that church. The personal comments were published in their church paper. He began by referring to comments made by his pastor in the pulpit and church paper "regarding the forces and attitudes that tend to polarize our congregation on national and international issues." Then my

116

friend Paul Behrens said, "I would like to add my two cents."

There is a small discussion group that has been meeting on Thursday evenings for several weeks to consider our Christian responsibility for total life stewardship. Ira Stephans and I are members of this group. Our discussions have gotten into major national and world problems. In many cases, Steve and I find that our views are in direct conflict. It is very disturbing to confront this deep difference of opinion with another man who is not only a long-time friend, but also a neighbor and fellow deacon.

These confrontations with Steve were disturbing enough that I began to wonder if it was worthwhile to continue in the discussion group. However, Dick Hardy's comments caused me to give this situation a lot of thought. I have finally concluded that these differences with Steve, rather than being a cause for quitting discussion, are probably the most important reason for continuing. If we can't meet as Christians—sharing a concern for mankind, and honestly discuss our differences, then where can we meet?

Throughout this country and around the world, people who hold differing views are confronting each other in the streets and across battle lines. Very often these people are clashing today with hatred and bloodshed because they, and preceding generations, have refused to sit down and discuss their differences.

You may feel that this doesn't apply to you. Perhaps you are proud of the fact that although you have your own opinions, you don't force them on others and see no need to discuss them. Well, can we really avoid confrontations? There are multitudes of people clamoring around us who are not as comfortable and well-fed and have fewer advantages. Can we afford not to respond to them? The world is talking to us from magazines, TV, newspapers, and pulpits. Can we turn a deaf ear?

Of course it is disturbing to confront those with whom we disagree; but if we are committed to right thinking, can we withhold our pet opinions from the abrasive action of free discussions?

Can we then meet with humility and compassion? Can we love and respect each other and be open to each other? If we would follow the example of Christ, can we do any less than this?

These are some of the signs of our times: the dangers of violence, the possibilities of reasonable discussion, and the necessity of providing compassion.

How do we read the weather? Where are we going to invest our energies during the days ahead?

13. WHEN JESUS DISCOVERED THAT RELIGION CAN BE FUN
Luke 10:21-24; 11:27-28

Can religion really be fun? Isn't being a Christian a serious business? Certainly one's religious faith is related to all that is of greatest meaning and has longest duration. Thus faith requires deep thought and earnest expression. Does this mean that our religious life must always be grave and somber?

Some people seem to behave on the supposition that just as soon as you give up enough pleasures you become religious. Such notions are quite different from Jesus' own life, which was filled with play and good humor. An eye-opening reading of the Gospels demonstrates that Jesus' own faith allowed him to appreciate the wit and humor of life. For Jesus, fun was not limited to only the trivial matters of life. Jesus' wit touched the deepest moments of his God-filled existence. A study of the Four Gospels shows, first, that even the most serious events of Jesus' life were touched by happy humor; second, that Jesus understood the essence of religion as joyous; and third, that for Jesus religion helped make life's burdens lighter. Let us consider each of the above statements at greater length.

What evidence is there for saying that Jesus showed a touch of humor and wit in some of the most serious events of his life? We have been aware of the sharp differences between Jesus and the religious leaders of his day. Perhaps we are so accustomed to reading about their clashes that we miss the way in which Jesus used humor to put down his opponents. Debaters know that humor in the hands of a clever opponent can be an effective weapon.

Consider the issue of the sabbath in Jesus' day: When Jesus was teaching in one of the synagogues, he noted a woman who was bent double. She had lived in this awkward position for eighteen years. Jesus cured her on the spot by calling to her, "Woman, you are released from your weakness" (Luke 13:12, Moffatt). Did the religious leaders appreciate the wonder of this healing act? No, they were offended that Jesus had relieved the woman of her physical impairment *on the sabbath day!* In Luke 13:14, Dr. Moffatt translated: "But the president of the synagogue was annoyed at Jesus healing on the sabbath, and he said to the crowd, 'There are six days for work to be done;

come during them to get healed, instead of the sabbath.' " Jesus' reply shows how humor can be used to expose the silliness of an argument. "The Lord replied to him, 'You hypocrite, does not each of you untether his ox or ass from the stall on the sabbath and lead it away to drink?' " (Luke 13:15, Moffatt).

Jesus first pictured a dumb animal tied to its stall. Even on the sabbath the religious code allowed such beasts to be led away to drink. This picture of untying the livestock formed the base for Jesus' play on words. " 'Now here is this descendant of Abraham whom Satan has kept in bonds for eighteen years; should she not be freed from her bonds on the Sabbath?' " (Luke 13:16, TEV). If you can untie your milk cow on the sabbath, why not a daughter of Abraham? If you are allowed to unhitch an animal, why not let this woman out of the old devil's corral? It really is a funny picture of the farmer in his sabbath finery leading the dumb ox to the water hole compared to the untying of this person. The humor of the contrast was not lost on his audience. You can almost hear the guffaws, and you can certainly sense the embarrassment of his vanquished opponents as Luke describes the situation. "His answer made all of his enemies ashamed of themselves, while all the people rejoiced over every wonderful thing that he did" (Luke 13:17, TEV). A speaker gets that kind of response only if he knows the worth of humor and makes the best use of it.

What wonderful helpers the Bible dictionaries are. Recommended is the article on "Humor" in *The Interpreter's Dictionary of the Bible*. Here the reader will find a distinction made between wit and humor. Wit has a snap to it, like the crack of a whip. Humor is slow and shy, moving lightly and capturing the imagination almost unawares. Both wit and humor involve perspective. Each takes something quite ordinary and allows us to smile or laugh as the commonplace is stretched out of shape. Wit captures our mind's eye as it instantly sizes up something that is out of place. Humor invades the intelligence by showing that what we take for granted as obvious often appears as ludicrous when seen with the playful eye.

The most common form of fun in the Bible is the pun. The people of Bible times shared our fondness for the clever turn of speech. Scholars have identified as many as five hundred word-plays in the Old Testament and two hundred in the New.[1]

[1] W. F. Stinespring, "Humor," *The Interpreter's Dictionary of the Bible*, ed. George A. Buttrick (Nashville: Abingdon Press, 1962), vol. E-J, pp. 660 f.

119

Jesus himself was quite good at this play on words. Because few moderns are at home in the Aramaic language Jesus spoke, we miss the exact turn of phrase, but we can come quite close.

The most obvious of Jesus' puns occurred in one of the most serious moments of his ministry. At Caesarea Philippi, Peter confessed that Jesus was truly the Messiah. Jesus responded, " 'And so I tell you: you are a rock, Peter, and on this rock I will build my church' " (Matthew 16:18, TEV). The play on the words *petra* for "rock" and *Petros*, "Peter," is an obvious one. The modern pun might sound like this: "You are Rocky and on this Rock I will build my church." The pun is fondly used by all men, great and small. It can easily be asserted that this particular play on words has had greater consequences than any other pun in the history of western man. Also this does not exhaust the humor that lies behind this solemn and sacred moment, for Jesus was well aware of Peter's character which really wasn't very much like a rock. The stuff Peter's personality was made of was more like slippery mercury than solid stone. Yet the truth of the pun was later confirmed in the rock-like faith of the apostle.

Let's turn to some other examples of Jesus' humor. To her chaplain, a co-ed caustically categorized a classmate: "She wears fancy dress, but underneath she has dirty lingerie." How similar this modern put-down is to the scathing picture Jesus painted of the religious people of his day: ". . . hypocrites! You clean the outside of cup and dish, which you have filled inside by robbery and self-indulgence!" (Matthew 23:25, NEB).

Jesus would have made a wonderful contributor to *MAD* magazine. This modern-day journal is a comic-book satire on present-day manners and morals. *MAD* cartoonists have poked fun at religious phonies as well as other foibles of society. It takes little imagination to visualize the cartoon figure of the pompous and pious creature Jesus describes: "So when you give something to a needy person, do not make a big show of it, as the show-offs do in the synagogues and on the streets" (Matthew 6:2, TEV).

Jesus' sense of humor allowed him to see how funny some people were as they tried to push themselves forward on the social scene. His perceptive eye caught the ridiculous element in such common scenes as the dinner guests who tried to find seats "above the salt." We sit with straight faces as we learn our lessons about hospitality and humility, but there was a gleam

120

in Jesus' watchful eyes as he watched the farce of diners elbowing their way to the head table. Perhaps we miss the satire in his social advice because we have heard it intoned from our pulpits so often. This paraphrase keeps the bite: "Now if you really want to get those front seats, sit back here until the host arrives. When he invites you to come on up front, then all the guests will notice your advancement to a place of honor." (Cf. Luke 14:7-10.) Of course in today's congregations Jesus might make some comments on the people who claim all the back rows. Are they just waiting for the invitation to come forward to occupy the front pews?

Jesus made many humorous comments on the social situation. These included the sketch of a cynical and corrupt judge who was more than outmatched by a stubborn and persistent woman (Luke 18:1-8). There is even a humorous twist in the profound lesson Jesus drew from this political cartoon. If a perverse magistrate will render a just verdict when insistently pressed to do so, how much more will a loving, heavenly Father listen to the constant prayers of the faithful?

Jesus was popular with the crowds that heard him because he was able to state profound truths in an imaginative way. He quickly spotted the incongruities of life and laid bare not only the nonsensical pretensions of men but also used the humorous occasion to lay open the religious dimensions of everyday existence. For instance, as he observed the various ways in which men practiced prayer, he sketched two intimate profiles for his listeners. First, he drew the picture of the righteous Pharisee. The man was selfless or certainly he thought himself to be so. He considered himself as honest as any one of his friends. Never had this devout man knowingly done an immoral deed! He regularly fasted and rigorously gave to charity. In his mirror this man found reflected a paragon of pious virtue. He was indeed a solid citizen. But the wretched sinner, what about him? Again, delicate humor allowed Jesus to draw a compassionate comparison. The tax collector recognized that he had no claims upon God at all and showed this by standing back out of the way, a real outsider. He felt his shame so deeply that he could not even lift up his head to heaven. He was whipped, and he understood his own tragic situation. The good man, the Pharisee, remained content with his own goodness; he certainly seemed satisfied by his own doing. The sinful man was the one who needed God's hand to give him satisfaction, and the prayers of this wretched creature were the prayers which were heard by a merciful God (Luke 18:9-14).

Another familiar story told by Jesus also shows his use of humor to communicate a profound truth. How his listeners must have chuckled as Jesus portrayed the two men building their houses! Even the smallest child recognizes that the first two efforts of the three little pigs would not stand up to the huffery and puffery of that old windbag, the big bad wolf. Charlie Chaplin created humor by portraying a poor little tramp whose clumsy falls delighted the audiences. What movie-goers didn't feel better just watching someone more clumsy and less adequate than themselves? So Jesus' audiences were opened up to hearing the punch line when he drew a comparison between the two builders. The sensible man dug a deep foundation, right down to bedrock. Wouldn't any sensible man build a house this way? Wouldn't we all build our foundation on rock? But what about that poor, foolish fellow who actually tried to build a house right on soft soil without even putting down a foundation? He really did that! Of course with the first real downpour of rain, the rushing waters carried away the fool's house (Luke 6:46-49; Matthew 7:24-27).

Contrasting the wise builder with the foolish man actually produces a delayed action form of humor. Some time after first hearing the story, you are thinking about that silly character and wondering how anybody could be so dumb. Then, like having your cat leap up onto you as you stand in your backyard, the truth pounces upon you. Jesus words actually involved us: "Why do you keep calling me 'Lord, Lord' — and never do what I tell you?" (Luke 6:46, NEB). There is more here than a story about a wise builder and a foolish boor; it catches our consciences. Humor is a delicate instrument, and Jesus was most skillful in its use.

Christianity today is identified with Europe and the Americas. We tend to forget that the Holy Land is located in Asia. Thus we often overlook the fact that Jesus and his audiences were Oriental in their thinking. The people of Bible times seem to have enjoyed hyperbole. Jesus certainly made good use of the exaggerated comic situation. He achieved dramatic as well as humorous results with it. Consider the discomfort of the man whose eye is irritated by a small speck. A helpful person, armed with a clean handkerchief and every good intention, offers to take the speck out from under his eyelid. It can be cleared up quite easily except for one minor complication. The would-be assistant has a twenty-foot telegraph pole jammed into his own eye (Matthew 7:3-5; Luke 6:41-42).

The humor of the situation Jesus pictured is similar to the experience a friend confided to me recently. Feeling a cold coming on, she went to see her doctor. When her physician entered the examining room, he barely managed to cover his own sneeze. With a faint, hoarse voice he rasped, "What can I do for you?" She wearily responded, "Not much, Doc." The day-to-day events of life do sometimes reveal humorous aspects, and Jesus spotted some of these outrageously out-of-place incidents.

A similarly extravagant picture is that of the meticulous person who carefully strains out the tiny gnat in order not to be defiled by something that is religiously unclean. Then this scrupulous observer of the dietary laws swallows a camel. Of course, the camel is also on the prohibited list, but it is so very big! In this grotesque image, Jesus pokes fun at the distortions so evident among the religious people of his day.

A similar contradiction is evident today among those who condemn going to movies and then go home to watch the late movies on television. Contradiction is also evident in an incident which happened in a small Oregon town. A drive-in specializing in fried fish used a picture of a mermaid on its outdoor display sign. The upper deck of the half female, half fish was a bare bosom. The citizens were upset by this breach of decency. It became a community crisis. While all the townspeople were in an uproar, the high school students were expressing their confusion to their teachers. Why this tremendous display of horror at a poorly painted figure when the town itself was plagued by problems of poverty, drugs, drunkenness, and family break-ups? The camel is still a forbidden favorite in the diets of the spiritually overstuffed. Jesus used exaggerated and humorous imagery to denounce the hypocrisies into which the religiously devout so often fall.

Jesus used the extravagant illustration very much as a modern political cartoonist does. The editorial page of many a modern newspaper has copied from the artistry of Jesus, who handily outwitted his opposition. Consider his portrayal of the political-religious bigwigs as ". . . whitewashed tombs, which look fine on the outside, but are full of dead men's bones and rotten stuff on the inside" (Matthew 23:27, TEV). Perhaps because of the serious nature of the controversy which eventually proved very costly to all concerned, we have missed the humorous dimensions of Jesus' verbal thrusts. It was because he was so effective in his use of humor that Jesus commanded such a large following. Perhaps because we have elevated the Gospels to such a high position of reverence, we miss the devastating humor which made Jesus such a threat to those entrenched in the seats of power. The crowds of his day were no different than modern-day crowds who roar their satisfaction when a political leader scores upon his opponent with an especially funny remark. Politicians of every age have had reason to fear the bite of a jest which exposes truth.

These different examples show the various ways in which Jesus used wit and humor. He was able to hook the imaginations of his hearers, denounce religious phonies, and defeat those who ganged up on him. He found numerous uses for good laughter. At the same time his use of humor also revealed his attitude toward life and religion.

Jesus found joy essential to good religion. Perhaps the reason Jesus felt free to employ humor even in serious moments was because he had discovered that religion was essentially an experience of joy. As we read the Four Gospels, we again and again come across religious happenings which are described as joyous events. We are aware of the accusation leveled against Jesus that he and his disciples were having too many good times. They were not behaving as soberly as religious types were supposed to behave! "Why is it that the disciples of John the Baptist and the disciples of the Pharisees fast, but yours do not?" (Mark 2:18, TEV). The reply Jesus made underlines the festive mood which marked his early ministry. "Can the wedding guests fast while the bridegroom is with them?" This note of celebration along with the fresh new approach he took was accentuated in the phrase Jesus used to close this exchange: "Fresh skins for new wine!" (Mark 2:22*c*, TEV). This atmosphere of merry celebration continued as Jesus sent his disciples out on their first missions. Luke describes how "the seventy-two men came back in great joy" (Luke 10:17*a*, TEV).

The wedding at Cana is another instance of Jesus enjoying himself at a party. For the religious person in Jesus' time the highest calling was the study of the Holy Scriptures. The Bible scholar, however, was admonished by the Talmud to leave his studies whenever he was invited to a wedding. The public decla-

124

ration of the founding of a new family unit was something special in the life of the human community. Certainly Jesus seemed to enjoy such conviviality.

This note of festivity and freedom is again being sounded at modern weddings. Young couples are rebelling against austere fashions of the past and want lively festivals when they publicly exchange their vows. They insist that their mutual pledges be said in a joy-filled atmosphere. Perhaps this is the reason that the bride and groom want a larger share in writing the marriage ceremony. They reject the pomp and solemnity that surrounded church rituals in the past. Weddings are happy events. Various youth movements today are trying to recapture the spontaneity of life remembered from happy childhood. Films, such as *Alice's Restaurant* and *Woodstock,* communicate this insistent longing for a joyful life. Jesus probably would have understood such "vibrations" as the young are sending out today.

However, to enjoy social occasions is not quite the same as finding joy in religion. So a closer look at what Jesus actually taught is in order. Jesus described the faith-invested life as the kingdom of God. The man of faith was the man who lived as God's citizen, obedient to the divine will. Such a faith-filled man took part in true happiness. As Jesus described it: ". . . how happy are those who hear the word of God and obey it!" (Luke 11:28, TEV). Rather than resulting from a deliberate effort "to have fun," such joy was a spontaneous surprise which overtook you as you pursued some other effort. The sense of joy suddenly came upon the distraught woman who was searching for the lost coin. The ten coins may have been part of the woman's headdress, worn on her wedding day. The symbol of her marriage was incomplete until she located the missing medal. The joy expressed by this woman when she found the missing coin was compared by Jesus to the rejoicing of the angels of God over the repentant sinner.

Joy is featured in another familiar parable. There was the shepherd who left the big flock of ninety-nine sheep huddled together, protected only by the sheep dogs, in order to go and search for the one stray. When the shepherd did find the straggler, ". . . he is so happy that he puts it on his shoulders, carries it back home, and calls his friends and neighbors together. 'Rejoice with me,' he tells them, 'for I have found my lost sheep!'" (Luke 15:5-6, TEV).

Joy is having a loved one you've been missing for a long time unexpectedly turn up. We are living in the age of the prodigal son. How many parents spend anxious lives concerned for the well-being of their absent children? Yet the business of life must go on. So the farm is tended, the stock watered and fed, and the establishment, such as it is, is maintained. Yet the father yearns to be reunited with the long-absent younger son. Happy is the day when the wasteful child, himself now wasted, turns up at his father's gates. Later the father explains to the hard-working elder brother: ". . . we had to have a feast and be happy, for your brother was dead, but now he is alive . . ." (Luke 15:32, TEV).

Our religious life can be like that, Jesus teaches us. To hold citizenship in God's kingdom is to have a passport to festivity and joyous celebration, and *not* to belong among God's people is death. To take part in God's kingdom is life. To be without citizenship is the occasion for grief and sadness. To hold citizenship is cause for festive gaiety. When the prodigal returns to his father's house, it is the right time for music and dancing.

Do we, as so many modern Christians, have a sad religion because we are not ready to admit that we have been prodigal, wandering far from our Father's house? Indeed, we do need to accept our Father's welcoming forgiveness. We are free to say, "Let's go in and join the party he is giving for us because we have come home!"

Or perhaps we have been working in our Father's house like a slave all these years. We really have tried to obey every single order he has given us. Why, then, is it so hard for us to hear what our Father is saying to the loyal, elder brother: "You are always at home and everything I have is yours" (Luke 15:31, TEV)? Everything God has is ours to use and to enjoy. Knowing this, we are free to bubble with delight and be filled with happiness! Such is Jesus' assurance to us. Faith fundamentally is joyous.

We have been examining the ways in which Jesus showed that being religious means having fun. We have seen the many different times when even the most serious events of his life were touched by a sense of humor. We have taken careful notice of his basic claim that the religious experience is a happy encounter. Now we turn to the third understanding that grows out of Jesus' discovery of fun as a dimension of faith.

Religion helps lighten the burdens of life. Why did this discovery that religion is a pleasure create a crisis in the life of

126

Jesus? Probably because Jesus concluded that faith in God makes life's burdens lighter. Putting really good news before his listeners added to the enmity Jesus already had acquired because the dominant religious faction of his day understood holiness in terms of demands, diets, and duties.

"You ought to do this — you must do that" is what so much of religion still sounds like. Whether in Jesus' time or our own, religion smacks of requirements. "That's a no-no," one college student said to a faculty member. Too much of our religious practices have been bullied by the "no-no" mentality. Thus one stereotype of the religious personality pictures an uptight square with O*U*G*H*T printed on his T-shirt. Why has this stereotype developed? Perhaps because so many admittedly religious persons have behaved in a starched-shirt manner and have seemed compulsive about the keeping of rules.

Jesus warned against phony role playing and pious pretense. "And when you fast, do not put on a sad face like the show-offs do. They go around with a hungry look so that everybody will be sure to see that they are fasting" (Matthew 6:16, TEV). Not only did Jesus attack such false parading, but he also was more harsh still with those who insisted on heavy rules. Jesus accused the scriptural experts of confusing religious living with strict conformity with regulations: "How terrible for you, too, teachers of the Law! You put loads on men's backs which are hard to carry, but you yourselves will not stretch out a finger to help them carry those loads" (Luke 11:46, TEV).

What did Jesus propose as essential religion? His invitation was: "Come to me, all of you who are tired from carrying your heavy loads, and I will give you rest" (Matthew 11:28, TEV). In place of the back-breaking burdens laid on by legalistic religion, Jesus offered refreshment: "Bend your necks to my yoke, and learn from me, for I am gentle and humble-hearted; and your souls will find relief. For my yoke is good to bear, my load is light" (Matthew 11:29-30, NEB).

Any time that a young upstart dares to suggest that religion is to be enjoyed and that faith is not just meeting a strict set of requirements, that young critic is certain to be tagged as a revolutionary. In Copenhagen, in the nineteenth century, the young Sören Kierkegaard lashed out against the artificial demands of what he derided as "Christendom." All of organized religion turned against the youthful philosopher and effectively pushed him outside of polite society.

127

In the first century the orthodox religious leaders were convinced that the way to please God was to meet severe restrictions. To such devout legalists Jesus' words about easy loads sounded more like a sad betrayal than basic religion. It is imperative that in our century religious believers not confuse the easy yoke of Jesus with "cheap grace." God does not forgive just because it is his business to forgive. That would be cheap grace, indeed. Rather, God's forgiveness rises out of his love for the sinner. God's caring concern makes reconciliation possible. Instead of regulations and pious practices, Jesus offers loving reunion. Such love is costly. Yes, it has its investment of effort and toil. But the burden is of a definitely different sort. The Lord offered himself as a servant to his disciples. Love which serves often must suffer. To be the waiting father of a wasteful, wandering son is no casual matter. But Jesus knew, and wants us to know, that if we will give ourselves in love for our fellowmen, God's love will reach under such a task, and our servant loads will be made lighter. The divine love provides a definite lift. His "yoke is kindly" (Matthew 11:30, Moffatt), and the soul that depends upon him is refreshed.

Because Jesus experienced religion as a joyous happening he also could promise his followers ". . . the kind of gladness that no one can take away from you" (John 16:22, TEV).

The many different examples drawn from his teachings show that Jesus did spice many of his more serious moments with a touch of humor. Certainly his message is verified in his own life which gives testimony that the faithful life is a joyous movement. Jesus communicated his assurance that life's burdens are made lighter through God's supportive love.

It is appropriate for the Christian to celebrate. We can be happy, for we have life and we share love. So we are enabled to encourage one another with a sense of spiritual buoyancy, "Have faith — have fun!"